The
High-Caste Hindu Woman

The
High-Caste Hindu Woman

By

PANDITA RAMABAI SARASVATI

With Introduction by The Board of Managers of the American Ramabai Association

GYAN

Published by

Gyan Publishing House
5, Ansari Road
Daryaganj, New Delhi-110002
Phone: 011-47034999, 9811692060
E-mail: books@gyanbooks.com

Distribution Network
gyanbooks.com
India, USA, Canada, UK, Australia, France

ISBN : 978-81-212-9796-7 (PB)
First Published, 1901

2nd Impression 2023

Printed at: Gyan Press, Delhi.

THE HIGH-CASTE HINDU WOMAN
Author: PANDITA RAMABAI SARASVATI

Ramabai

The

High-Caste Hindu Woman

By

PANDITA RAMABAI SARASVATI

With Introduction by The Board of Managers of the American Ramabai Association

A NEW EDITION

1901

TO THE

MEMORY OF MY BELOVED MOTHER,

LAKSHMÎBAI DONGRE,

WHOSE SWEET INFLUENCE AND ABLE INSTRUCTION

HAVE BEEN

THE LIGHT AND GUIDE OF MY LIFE,

THIS LITTLE VOLUME

IS MOST REVERENTLY DEDICATED.

CONTENTS

LIST OF ILLUSTRATIONS

Introduction

DURING the past year so many have been the calls for Pandita Ramabai's "High-Caste Hindu Woman" published in 1887 that the Board of Managers of the American Ramabai Association think a reprint of the book advisable. To this Ramabai gives her consent, with the request that the Introduction by Dean Bodley be omitted, for which the Managers substitute a condensed account of her life and experiences from childhood to the present time. To many who have read the reports of the Executive Committee from year to year this will be a familiar story—reports based upon the official correspondence and personal interviews with Ramabai during the past thirteen years. Facts so authenticated by Ramabai's own lips and pen cannot be too often repeated. Here, in justice to the author of "The High-Caste Hindu Woman," a statement should be made that she does not make. It is that in her citations from Manu, the great Hindu law-giver, she not only had at her command the best translations of the sacred texts, but a thorough knowledge of the Sanskrit language which enabled her to make her own translations from the original. On her return from England and America, in appreciation of her great learning, one of her countrymen paid her the following tribute:—" Pandita Ramabai combines in herself what even in the men of India is a rare combination; a deep knowledge of the Hindu Shastras and an intimate acquaintance with the inner life, thought and speech of the most advanced and civilized nations of the West. For several centuries a lady Sanyasi so learned and so devoted to the elevation of her sex has not appeared on the stage of Indian life."

Forty-three years ago, on the 23rd of April, 1858, in the forest of Gungamal, in the Western Ghauts of India, a child was born, who as a woman was to stand forth alone, a fearless champion of the rights of her unfortunate sisters, to strike from them the chains of ignorance and superstition that for centuries have kept them in cruel bondage. Her parents gave to her the name of the goddess Rama, which signifies "bright." Her father, Ananta Shastri, a learned Brahman, taking to himself an ignorant child-wife nine years of age, resolved to put in practice his liberal theories concerning female education. But so horrified were his people by this open disregard of the cherished traditions and customs of the country that he was obliged to make for himself and his little wife Lakshmibai a home in the forest, where he could teach her unmolested save by the wild beasts. Her early memories of that home were of lying on the ground night after night, convulsed with terror by the cries of the beasts in the jungle, her husband sitting by her side to soothe her. Day by day the lessons went on; her gifted mind responded readily to her husband's teachings; in time she realized his fondest hopes, and became the teacher of the children who came to them.

Ramabai's still vivid memories of the forest home are of being awakened at early dawn by a mother's tender caress, and of the early morning lessons learned only from her mother's lips and from Nature. Not long after her birth the life of the family became a wandering one, consisting of homes in forests, long pilgrimages, traveling from city to city, from town to town, often shelterless at night and hungry by day, the father still pleading fearlessly for the elevation of his countrywomen. Because of his advanced views concerning female education, and because he would not give his little daughter in marriage at the age of nine, he was virtually ostracized by his brethren. During this time Ramabai's education went on; she learned to speak Marathi, Hindustani, Kanarese and Bengali, and gained a wonderful knowledge of Sanskrit.

After the death of the parents, which occurred during the great famine of 1877, Ramabai and her brother took up the work of the father. Ramabai's fame as a lecturer reaching the ears of the pandits of Calcutta, they desired to hear and see for themselves. She obeyed their summons to appear before them; so astonished and pleased were they by the clearness of her views, and her eloquence in presenting them, that they publicly conferred on her the highest title—Sarasvati, Goddess of Wisdom.

It was during these wanderings with her brother that Ramabai's faith in the Hindu religion was shaken though she continued the worship of idols until nearly twenty years old. Conversations with Keeshub Chunder Sen, with the books he gave her to read, enlightened her in regard to other religions, and in a great measure prepared her for the acceptance of Christianity some years later. Although even at the time of her brother's death when left alone in the world, and again when overcome with grief by the sudden loss of her husband, she had a dim consciousness of being cared for by an Infinite Being who had no kinship with idols. In the pathetic account of her father's death Ramabai says that he did not know the only true God, but served the—to him—unknown God with all his heart. His last words to her were,—"Remember that you are my youngest, my best beloved child. I have given you into God's hands. You must serve Him all your life." Ramabai adds—"My father's prayers were heard by the Heavenly Father whom the old Hindu did not know, and I can now say to the departed spirit, 'Yes, dear father, I will serve the only true God to the last.'"

While journeying from city to city, from village to village, Ramabai, being a Brahman, had free access to the homes of the high-caste Hindus, saw the home life in all its cruel details, the misery of the child wife, the torture of the child widow, and resolved to devote her life to the redemption of her unfortunate sisters, especially the little widows.

After four years of close comradeship the brother died leaving Ramabai utterly alone and unprotected; but he died happier in the thought that there might be a Good God who would care for her. In her loneliness and grief she met Bipin Bihari Medhavi, a Bengali lawyer, a graduate from the Calcutta University, who fully sympathized with her in her liberal views and unselfish plans. They loved, married, and were happy, made more happy by the birth of a little daughter

RAMABAI AND MANORAMA [illegible]

—the blessing most desired—whom they named Mano (Hearts' Joy). As they were about to establish a small school for child-widows in their own home, the husband suddenly died, leaving Ramabai that most hapless of all women, a *sonless widow.*

Drinking again from the cup of sorrow now filled to overflowing Ramabai felt herself drawn nearer to God. The one sacred tie left to her—mother and child—did but intensify the mother-love and tenderness for the millions of child-wives and child-widows who had never tasted the joys of childhood, and she consecrated herself anew to their redemption. Feeling the need of greater knowledge and better training for her life work she resolved to seek them in England.

In May, 1883, Ramabai landed in England, a stranger to the people, its customs and language. She found a warm welcome and home with the Sisters of St. Mary's Home, at Wantage, and soon acquired a knowledge of the English language. She was then appointed Professor of Sanskrit in the Cheltenham Female College, where she studied natural science, higher mathematics, English literature and Greek.

In Ramabai's English study of the New Testament, she felt the truths of Christianity, gladly embraced them, and was baptized in the Episcopal Church, although then as now, entirely unsectarian in her belief. Her theology was "The Apostle's Creed—The Lord's Prayer—The Ten Commandments."

During nearly three years Ramabai pursued the educational course of teaching and study as a preparation for her life work, for which she had then no formulated plans. Therefore an unexpected invitation to attend the graduation of her cousin, Dr. Joshee, from the Woman's Medical College in Philadelphia, seemed to her to be "the call of God." She came in February, 1886, and was taken into the home and heart of Dean Rachel L. Bodley, who encouraged her to remain, and mature her plans in America. In the public school system, the kindergarten and industrial training, she found the solution of her problem.

After writing "The High-Caste Hindu Woman"—the proceeds from which were to be devoted to compiling her Marathi school-books; after studying the public-school systems and taking a thorough course of kindergarten training, she made her appeals to the people to aid her in establishing a secular school for the high-caste child-widows who could not be reached in other ways. The appeals were to men and women of every denomination. She asked, moreover, that they should form themselves into an Association to be the custodian of the funds that might be given her, and to which she should be responsible for the use of those funds.

May 28, 1887, at a public meeting held in Boston, a provisional committee was appointed to consider Ramabai's plan, to act as far as possible, and to report at a later meeting. In December they presented a report that was accepted, officers were elected, a constitution was adopted, and the temporary Association became an organization—it seemed to spring into existence, and Ramabai saw her long cherished plan take definite form. That night her joy was too great for sleep; when found sobbing in her room, she explained, "I am crying for joy that my dream of years has become a reality." The officers of the Association were Rev. Dr. Edward Everett Hale, President; Vice-Presidents, Rev. Dr. Phillips Brooks, Rev. Dr. Lyman Abbott, Rev. Dr. George A. Gordon, Mrs. Mary Hemenway, Dean Rachel L. Bodley, and Frances E. Willard—a rare body of officers—Unitarian, Episcopalian, Orthodox, Baptist and Methodist. The Board of Trustees, consisting of some of the best business men and professional men of Boston, and the Executive Committee of philanthropic women, were equally undenominational. The Association pledged itself to the support of a secular school for ten years—a school in which no religious instruction either Hindu or Christian should be given. The Bible and the Vedas were to stand side by side in the school library, free to all. The caste rules were to be observed, but there were to be no public religious observances of any kind. This was Ramabai's pledge to her own and the American people, which pledge she kept inviolate.

After the formation of the Association Ramabai considered herself its servant. From May, 1887, to November, 1888, this dauntless little woman of thirty, in the midst of a strange people, strange customs and manners, eating neither "fish, flesh nor fowl," drinking nothing stronger than water and milk, often cold and hungry, showed a degree of mental and physical endurance that was marvellous even in the eyes of an American.

Protected from insult by her pure womanliness and strong personality, she traveled from Canada to the Pacific Coast, lecturing, forming Circles, studying educational, philanthropic and charitable institutions, omitting nothing that might prove helpful to her people. Reaching the Pacific Coast, her impassioned appeals enlisted the sympathy of ministers of all creeds—Protestant, Catholic and Hebrew—of earnest women and business men, and an auxiliary Association was there formed that sent to the treasury the first year $5,000. In November, 1888, with an assured annual income sufficient for the support of a secular school of fifty pupils for ten years, Ramabai bade good-by to a land that had grown very dear to her, and turned her face homewards bright with hope, and with a brave heart, though she knew not how her countrymen would receive her.

February 1st, 1889, she again stood on the shores of her native land after an absence of nearly six years, her return warmly welcomed by many of her countrymen. In less than six weeks a school was opened in Bombay with two pupils, one of whom had thrice attempted suicide, restrained only by the fear of being born again a woman.

The school was named Shâradâ Sadan—Home of Wisdom—for it was indeed a home as well as a school. In twelve months it had gained in reputation and numbers far beyond the expectations of its most sanguine friends. It was soon removed to Poona, the "stronghold of Brahmanism," where it has enjoyed blessed sunshine and

SHÂRADÂ SADAN AT BOMBAY

encountered fierce storms. Once only did Ramabai yield to the pressure upon mind and body. This was in 1893 when it seemed almost impossible for the school to withstand the attacks made upon it and the withdrawal of many of its pupils, or for Ramabai to endure the desertion of old and dear friends, the unexpected cruel accusations made against her, and the sight of her high hopes for her suffering sisters seemingly coming to naught. But God and the right were on her side, and she came forth from the trial more hopeful than ever.

It was at this time, and because of this storm, that the Chairman of the Executive Committee visited the school. She interviewed friends and the unfriendly, members of the Advisory Board, parents, teachers and pupils, and found all the accusations against Ramabai groundless. But the knowledge she gained of the social evils of the country was appalling. From the educated Hindus visiting Ramabai's school she learned much. Mingling with the high-caste child-widows day after day, month after month, she read signs of past suffering in the sad eyes of many, and from the lips of others heard tales of cruelty such as would rouse pity and indignation in the most indifferent heart. Could Ramabai's private records be given to the public the stoutest heart might quail before the revelations of physical torture, and of temptations more fearful than torture, sometimes yielded to, sometimes bravely withstood.

It was not long before the old pupils began to return and new ones to arrive; old friends renewed their loyalty and new ones were gained; and Ramabai, with her indomitable will and unparalleled courage, rallied from prostration and depression. With the renewed prosperity of the school she began to dream dreams and see visions of making it self-supporting when the support of the American people should cease. Hearing of a farm not far from Poona that could be purchased very reasonably if secured at once, she conceived the plan of planting it with mango trees, orange trees and vegetables, which she estimated would in five years give an income of

$5,000. Her letter applying for $4,000, the sum required for the purchase, was so clear, concise and business-like that it was with regret the Trustees felt obliged to refuse on the ground that the Association funds could not be legally used for that purpose. Copies of the letter were sent to a few of her American friends with the result that is better told in her own graphic words written to the Executive Committee:—"After receiving your cablegram I went to Bombay hoping to raise money on my life insurance, but failed. During the trip home my heart was rebellious that I could not have rupees sufficient to secure that farm, when I saw a little sparrow on a branch undismayed by the noise of the train. I thought of what the Bible said of the 'sparrow' and felt ashamed of my lack of faith. Reaching home I told the teachers I had failed, but that we had a rich Father in Heaven who would yet give us that farm. Not long after I was awakened very early in the morning and a cablegram from America was placed in my hand. I trembled, fearing I knew not what, but raised my heart in prayer to God to help me bear whatever the cablegram contained. I opened it and the farm was mine!" The prompt and generous responses of half-a-dozen friends enabled the treasurer to send the sum needed to secure the farm in less than six weeks after the letter was received. Two generous friends were in Florence when a copy of the letter reached them, the reply to which was a cablegram authorizing $2,000 to be sent to Ramabai at once. The farm was purchased and quickly put under cultivation, circles and individuals contributing the means for stocking it. It was supplying the Shârādâ Sadan with vegetables and sending a surplus to market, while the dairy was providing milk more than sufficient for the school, when the famine of 1897 occurred, during which time the farm proved a blessing far beyond Ramabai's dreams.

Unable to resist the pleadings of her own heart, she went to the famine district herself, rescued three hundred high-caste girls from sin and death, and brought them to the Shârādâ Sadan. The beautiful compound was turned into a camping-

CARRYING WATER IN CARTS AT MUKTI

ground, and the poor girls were cared for by Ramabai, teachers, and pupils, until the plague obliged them to leave Poona, when the farm to which they were removed proved their "salvation" indeed. Ramabai at once began to dig wells, erect buildings, and start industries for the new pupils; and she called this Christian home "Mukti" (Salvation). The next year, 1898, when the ten years' pledge had expired, at the request of the Association Ramabai came to America again. At the annual meeting, March 16th, the marvellous success of the ten years' experience was briefly stated. During that time the Association received from circles and individuals $95,531, and owned property worth $50,000, which property it still owns in accordance with Ramabai's wish. During nine school years fourteen pupils had been trained as teachers, nine of whom were in good positions, and two had opened schools of their own. Of eight trained as nurses five were employed. Seven were matrons, two were housekeepers, and ten had happy homes of their own. Of the three hundred and fifty who had been in the Sadan for a longer or shorter time forty-eight had become Christians through the unconscious influence of Ramabai's daily life, twenty-three of whom were voluntary Christian workers, all retaining the Hindu customs and costumes. Then followed Ramabai's story of her enlarged work, the result of the famine and the pestilence.

With her thrilling word-pictures of the sufferings of the famine children she stirred the hearts of her hearers anew. With even more confidence than when ten years before she appealed to the public for an Association and an annual income of $5,000, she now asked for a reorganized Association and $20,000 annually. Her prayers have been richly answered. The Association was organized and incorporated under the name of "The American Ramabai Association," and through it she has received during the past three years $50,256, $22,000 of which were remittances between March 1, 1900, and March 1, 1901. But with the utmost vigilance and strictest economy her needs are many and great. Several times since her return has she

MANORAMA

taken her life in her hands, gone to the famine districts and rescued hundreds of child-widows and deserted wives from physical and moral death, until her family numbers nearly two thousand, over which she has the entire control.

The Shâradâ Sadan which is still secular and gives the higher education, and the Mukti, a Christian and industrial school, are sister institutions in which Ramabai is preparing her children for useful, self-supporting, self-respecting, happy lives. In this work she soon will be ably seconded by her daughter who was graduated with honor last June at the A. M. Chesbrough Seminary, North Chili, New York. Unselfishly putting aside her desire for a college course Manorama returned to India last fall—the fall of 1900—to relieve her mother and to learn the details of the work. She is happy and successful as the Vice-Principal of the Shâradâ Sadan.

The conception, the inception, the development, and marvellous success of these schools are due to the self-consecration of one woman—a child of God working for and with Him for the relief of her suffering sisters, and the uplifting of her people—and that woman a Hindu widow!

When fourteen years ago Ramabai was asked for a message to the readers of "The High-Caste Hindu Woman," she replied: "Remind them that it was out of Nazareth that the blessed Redeemer of mankind came; that great reforms have again and again been wrought by instrumentalities that the world despised. Ask them to help me educate the high-caste child-widow; for I solemnly believe that this hated and despised class of women, educated and enlightened, are by God's grace to redeem India."

Fourteen years ago God put into the hearts and hands of the American people the desire and the power to grant Ramabai's prayer; to help inaugurate and carry forward this unparalleled work. Will they let it languish now? Will American husbands and fathers, will American wives and mothers, will the children of this Christian land, turn a deaf ear to the cry of millions of India's suffering children? Will they shut their eyes and close their ears to the sights and sounds that are still filling Ramabai's heart with pain unutterable? No, they will not, for it is the loving Father of all Who calls upon them to give to this heroic woman their loving sympathy and generous aid.

For the Board of Managers,

JUDITH W. ANDREWS,

Chairman of the Executive Committee.

BOSTON, *April* 23, 1901.

The High-Caste Hindu Woman

I

PREFATORY REMARKS

In order to understand the life of a Hindu woman, it is necessary for the foreign reader to know something of the religion and the social customs of the Hindu nation. The population of Hindustan numbers two hundred and fifty millions, and is made up of Hindus, Mahometans, Eurasians, Europeans and Jews; more than three-fifths of this vast population are professors of the so-called Hindu religion in one or the other of its forms. Among these the religious customs and orders are essentially the same; the social customs differ slightly in various parts of the country, but they have an unmistakable similarity underlying them.

The religion of the Hindus is too vast a subject to be fully treated in a few paragraphs; it may be briefly stated, however, somewhat thus:—All Hindus recognize the Vedas and other apocryphal books as the canonical scriptures. They believe in one supreme spirit, Paramatma, which is pure, passionless, omnipresent, holy and formless in its essence, but when it is influenced by Maya, or illusion, it assumes form, becomes male and female, creates every thing in the universe out of its own substance. A Hindu, therefore, does not think it a sin to worship rivers, mountains, heavenly bodies, creatures, etc., since they are all consubstantial with God and manifestations of the same spirit. Any one of these manifestations may be selected to be the object of devotion, according to a man's own choice; his favorite divinity he will call the supreme ruler of the universe, and the others gods, servants of the supreme ruler.

Hindus believe in the immortality of the soul, inasmuch as it is consubstantial with God; man is rewarded or punished according to his deeds.

He undergoes existences of different descriptions in order to reap the fruit of his deeds. When at length he is free from the consequences of his action, which he can be by knowing the Great Spirit as it is and its relation to himself, he is then re-absorbed into the spirit and ceases to be an individual; just as a river ceases to be different from the ocean when it flows into the sea.

According to this doctrine, a man is liable to be born eight million four hundred thousand times before he can become a Brahman (first caste), and except one be a Brahman he is not fit to be re-absorbed into the spirit, even though he obtain the true knowledge of the Paramatma. It is, therefore, necessary for every person of other castes to be careful not to transgress the law by any imprudent act, lest he be again subjected to be born eight million four hundred thousand times. A Brahman must incessantly try to attain to the perfection of the supreme knowledge, for it is his last chance to get rid of the misery of the long series of earthly existences; the least trifling transgression of social or religious rules however renders him liable to the degradation of perpetual births and deaths.

These, with the caste beliefs, are the chief articles of the Hindu creed at the present day. There are a few heterodox Hindus who deny all this; they are pure theists in their belief, and disregard all idolatrous customs. These Bramos, as they are called, are doing much good by purifying the national religion.

As regards social customs, it may be said that the daily life and habits of the people are immensely influenced by religion in India. There is not an act that is not performed religiously by them; a humorous author has said, with some truth, that "the Hindus even sin religiously." The rising from the bed in the morning, the cleaning of teeth, washing of hands and bathing of the body, the wearing of garments, lighting the fire or the lamp, eating and drinking and every act of similar description, is done in a prescribed manner, and with the utterance of prayers or in profound silence. Each custom, when it is old enough to be entitled "the way of the ancients," takes the form of religion and is scrupulously observed. These customs, founded for the most part on tradition, are altogether independent of the canonical writings, so much so that a person is liable to be punished, or even excommunicated, for doing a deed forbidden by custom, even though it be sanctioned by religion.

For example, eating the food prepared by persons of an inferior caste is not only not forbidden by the sacred laws, but is sanctioned by them.*

At the present day, however, time-honored custom overrules the ancient laws, and says that a person must not eat anything cooked nor drink water polluted by the touch of a person of inferior caste. Hindus transgressing this rule

---

* "Pure men of the first three castes shall prepare the food of a householder" (Brahman or other high caste).

"Or Shudras (servile caste) may prepare the food under the superintendence of men of the first three castes."—*Apastamba* II. 2, 3. 1, 4.

instantly forfeit their caste, and must undergo some heavy penance to regain it.

Without doubt, "caste" originated in the economical division of labor. The talented and most intelligent portion of the Aryan Hindus became, as was natural, the governing body of the entire race. They, in their wisdom, saw the necessity of dividing society, and subsequently set each portion apart to undertake certain duties which might promote the welfare of the nation. The priesthood (Brahman caste) were appointed to be the spiritual governors over all, and were the recognized head of society. The vigorous, warlike portion of the people (Kshatriya, or warrior caste) was to defend the country, and suppress crime and injustice by means of physical strength; assisted by the priesthood, they were to be the temporal governors in the administration of justice. The business-loving tradesmen and artisans (Vaisya, or trader caste) had also an important position assigned under the preceding classes or castes. The fourth, or servile class (Shudra caste) was made up of all those not included in the preceding three castes. In ancient times persons were assigned to each of the four castes according to their individual capacity and merit, independent of the accident of birth.

Later on, when caste became an article of the Hindu faith, it assumed the formidable proportions which now prevail everywhere in India. A son of a Brahman is honored as the head of all castes, not because of his merit, but because he was born into a Brahman family. Intermarriage of castes was once recognized as lawful, even after caste by inheritance had been acknowledged, provided that a woman of superior caste did not marry a man of an inferior caste; but now law is overruled by custom. Intermarriages cannot take place without involving serious consequences, and making the offenders outcasts.

The four principal castes* are again divided into clans; men belonging to high clans must

* "There are four castes—Brahmanas, Kshatriyas, Vaisyas, and Shudras."

"Amongst these, each preceding caste is superior by birth to the one following."—*Apastamba* I. 1, 1, 3, 4.

not give their daughters in marriage to men of low clans. To transgress this custom is to lose family honor, caste privileges, and even intercourse with friends and relatives.

Besides the four castes and their clans there are numerous castes called collectively, "mixed castes" formed by the intermarriage of members of the preceding; their number is again increased by castes according to employment, as scribe, tanner, cobbler, shoemaker, tailor, etc., etc. Even the outcasts, such for example as the sweeper, have their own distinctions, as powerful among themselves as are those of the high castes. Transgressors of caste rules are, from the highest to the lowest, subject to excommunication and severe punishment. Offenders by intermarriage, or change of faith, are without redemption. It must also be borne in mind, that if a Brahman condescends to marry a person of lower caste, or eats and drinks with any of them, he is de-

"The Brahmana, the Kshatriya and the Vaisya castes are the twice-born ones, but the fourth, the Shudra, has one birth only; there is no fifth caste."—*Manu* X. 4.

spised and shunned as an outcast, not only by his own caste, but also by the low-caste with whose members he has entered into such relation. The low-caste people will look upon this Brahman as a lawless wretch. So deeply rooted is this custom in the heart of every orthodox Hindu that he is not in any way offended by the disrespect shown him by a high-caste man, since he recognizes in it only what is ordered by religion. For, although "caste" is confessedly an outgrowth of social order, it has now become the first great article of the Hindu creed all over India. Thoughtful men like Buddha, Nanak, Chaitanya and others rebelled against this tyrannical custom, and proclaimed the gospel of social equality of all men, but "caste" proved too strong for them. Their disciples at the present day are as much subject to caste as are any other orthodox Hindus. Even the Mahomedans have not escaped this tyrant; they, too, are divided into several castes, and are as strict as the Hindus in their observances. Over a million Hindu converts to Christianity, members of the Roman

Catholic Church, are more or less ruled by caste. The Protestant missionaries, likewise, found it difficult in early days to overcome caste prejudice among their converts, and not many years ago, in the Madras presidency, clergymen were compelled to use different cups for each separate caste when they celebrated the Lord's Supper.

The Vedas are believed by the devout Hindu to be the eternal, self-existing Word of God, revealed by Him to different sages. Besides the Vedas there are more than twenty-five books of sacred law, ascribed to different inspired authors who wrote or compiled them at various times, and on which are based the principal customs and religious institutes of the Hindus. Among these, the code of Manu ranks highest, and is believed by all to be very sacred, second to none but the Vedas themselves.

Although Manu and the other law-givers differ greatly on many points, they all agree on things concerning women. According to this sacred law a woman's life is divided into three parts, viz.:—1st, Childhood; 2nd, Youth or married life; 3rd, Widowhood or old age.

NOTE.—The translations of the sacred texts quoted throughout this work are those found in the well-known "Sacred Books of the East," edited by Prof. Max Müller, Clarendon Press, Oxford.

II

CHILDHOOD

ALTHOUGH the code of Manu contains a single passage in which it is written "A daughter is equal to a son," (See *Manu* IX. 130), the context expressly declares that equality to be founded upon the results attainable through her son; the passage therefore cannot be regarded as an exception to the statement that the ancient code establishes the superiority of male children. A son is the most coveted of all blessings that a Hindu craves, for it is by a son's birth in the family that the father is redeemed.

"Through a son he conquers the worlds, through a son's son he obtains immortality, but through his son's grandson he gains the world of the sun."—*Manu*, IX. 137.

"There is no place for a man (in Heaven) who is destitute of male offspring."—*Vasishtha*, XVII. 2.

If a man is sonless, it is desirable that he should have a daughter, for her son stands in the place of a son to his grandfather, through whom the grandfather may obtain salvation.

"Between a son's son and the son of a daughter there exists in this world no difference; for even the son of a daughter saves him who has no sons, in the next world, like the son's son."—*Manu*, IX. 139.

In Western and Southern India when a girl or a woman salutes the elders and priests, they bless her with these words—"Mayst thou have eight sons, and may thy husband survive thee." In the form of a blessing the deity is never invoked to grant daughters. Fathers very seldom wish to have daughters, for they are thought to be the property of somebody else; besides, a daughter is not supposed to be of any use to the parents in their old age. Although it is necessary for the continuance of the race that some girls should be born into the world, it is desirable that their number by no means should exceed that of the boys. If unfortunately a wife happens to have all daughters and no son, Manu authorizes the husband of such a woman to supersede her with another in the eleventh year of their marriage.*

In no other country is the mother so laden with care and anxiety on the approach of childbirth as in India. In most cases her hope of winning her husband to herself hangs solely on her bearing sons.

Women of the poorest as well as of the richest families, are almost invariably subjected to this trial. Many are the sad and heart-rending stories heard from the lips of unhappy women who have lost their husband's favor by bringing forth daughters only, or by having no children at all. Never shall I forget a sorrowful scene that I witnessed in my childhood. When about thirteen years of age I accompanied my mother and sister to a royal harem where they had been invited to pay a visit. The Prince had four wives, three of whom were childless. The eldest having been blessed with two sons, was of course the favorite of her husband, and her face beamed with happiness.

* See page 87.

SHÂRADÂ SADAN AT POONA

We were shown into the nursery and the royal bed-chamber, where signs of peace and contentment were conspicuous. But oh! what a contrast to this brightness was presented in the apartments of the childless three. Their faces were sad and careworn; there seemed no hope for them in this world, since their lord was displeased with them, on account of their misfortune.

A lady friend of mine in Calcutta told me that her husband had warned her not to give birth to a girl, the first time, or he would never see her face again, but happily for this wife and for her husband also, she had two sons before the daughter came. In the same family there was another woman, the sister-in-law of my friend, whose first-born had been a daughter. She longed unceasingly to have a son, in order to win her husband's favor, and when I went to the house, constantly besought me to foretell whether this time she should have a son! Poor woman! she had been notified by her husband that if she persisted in bearing daughters she should be superseded by another wife, have coarse clothes to wear and scanty food to eat, should have no ornaments, save those which are necessary to show the existence of a husband, and she should be made the drudge of the whole household. Not unfrequently, it is asserted, that bad luck attends a girl's advent, and poor superstitious mothers in order to avert such a catastrophe, attempt to convert the unborn child into a boy, if unhappily it be a girl.

Rosaries used by mothers of sons are procured to pray with; herbs and roots celebrated for their virtue are eagerly and regularly swallowed; trees and son-giving gods are devoutly worshipped. There is a curious ceremony, honored with the name of "sacrament," which is administered to the mother between the third and the fourth month of her pregnancy for the purpose of converting the embryo into a boy.

In spite of all these precautions girls will come into Hindu households as ill-luck, or rather nature, will have it. After the birth of one or more sons girls are not unwelcome, and under such circumstances, mothers very often long to have a daughter. And after her birth both parents lavish love and tenderness upon her, for natural affection, though modified and blunted by cruel custom, is still strong in the parent's heart. Especially may this be the case with the Hindu mother. That maternal affection, sweet and strong, before which "there is neither male nor female," asserts itself not unfrequently in Hindu homes, and overcomes selfishness and false fear of popular custom. A loving mother will sacrifice her own happiness by braving the displeasure of her lord, and will treat her little daughter as the best of all treasures. Such heroism is truly praiseworthy in a woman; any country might be proud of her. But alas! the dark side is too conspicuous to be passed over in silence.

In a home shadowed by adherence to cruel custom and prejudice, a child is born into the world; the poor mother is greatly distressed to learn that the little stranger is a daughter, and the neighbors turn their noses in all directions to manifest their disgust and indignation at the occurrence of such a phenomenon. The innocent babe is happily unconscious of all that is going on around her, for a time at least. The mother, who has lost the favor of her husband and relatives because of the girl's birth, may selfishly avenge herself by showing disregard to infantile needs and slighting babyish requests. Under such a mother the baby soon begins to feel her misery, although she does not understand how or why she is caused to suffer this cruel injustice.

If a girl is born after her brother's death, or if, soon after her birth, a boy in the family dies, she is in either case regarded by her parents and neighbors as the cause of the boy's death. She is then constantly addressed with some unpleasant name, slighted, beaten, cursed, persecuted and despised by all. Strange to say, some parents, instead of thinking of her as a comfort left to them, find it in their hearts, in the constant manifestation of their grief for the dear lost boy, to address the innocent girl with words such as these: "Wretched girl, why didst thou not die instead of our darling boy? Why didst thou crowd him out of the house by coming to us; or why didst not thou thyself become a boy?" "It would have been good for all of us if thou hadst died and thy brother lived!" I have myself several times heard parents say such things to their daughters, who, in their turn, looked sadly and wonderingly into the parents' faces, not comprehending why such cruel speeches should be heaped upon their heads when they had not done any harm to their brothers. If there is a boy remaining in the family, all the caresses and sweet words, the comforts and gifts, the blessings and praises are lavished upon him by parents and neighbors, and even by servants, who fully sympathize with the parents in their grief. On every occasion the poor girl is made to feel that she has no right to share her brother's good fortune, and that she is an unwelcome, unbidden guest in the family.

Brothers, in most cases, are, of course, very proud of their superior sex; they can know no better than what they see and hear concerning their own and their sisters' qualities. They, too, begin by and by to despise girls and women. It is not a rare thing to hear a mere slip of a boy gravely lecture his elder sister as to what she should or should not do, and remind her that she is only a girl and that he is a boy. Subjected to such humiliation, most girls become sullen, morbid and dull. There are some fiery natures, however, who burn with indignation, and burst out in their own childish eloquence; they tell their brothers and cousins that they soon are going to be given in marriage, and that they will not come to see them, even if they are often entreated to do so. Children, however, soon forget the wrong done them; they laugh, they shout, they run about freely, and are generally merry when unpleasant speeches are not showered upon them. Having little or no education, except a few prayers and popular songs to commit to memory, the little girls are mostly left to themselves, and they play in whatever manner they please. When about six or seven years of age they usually begin to help their mothers in household work, or in taking care of the younger children.

I have mentioned earlier the strictness of the

modern caste system in regard to marriage. Intelligent readers may, therefore, have already guessed that this reason lies at the bottom of the disfavor shown to girls in Hindu homes. From the first moment of the daughter's birth, the parents are tormented incessantly with anxiety in regard to her future, and the responsibilities of their position. Marriage is the most expensive of all Hindu festivities and ceremonies. The marriage of a girl of a high caste family involves an expenditure of two hundred dollars at the very least. Poverty in India is so great that not many fathers are able to incur this expense; if there are more than two daughters in a family, his ruin is inevitable. For, it should be remembered, the bread-winner of the house in Hindu society not only has to feed his own wife and children, but also his parents, his brothers unable to work either through ignorance or idleness, their families and the nearest widowed relatives, all of whom very often depend upon one man for their support; besides these, there are the family priests, religious beggars and others, who expect much from him. Thus, fettered hand and foot by barbarously cruel customs which threaten to strip him of everything he has, starvation and death staring him in the face, the wretched father of many girls is truly an object of pity. Religion enjoins that every girl must be given in marriage; the neglect of this duty means for the father unpardonable sin, public ridicule and caste excommunication. But this is not all. The girl must be married within a fixed period, the caste of the future husband must be the same, and the clan either equal or superior, but never inferior, to that of her father.

The Brahmans of Eastern India have observed successfully their clan prejudice for hundreds of years despite poverty; they have done this in part by taking advantage of the custom of polygamy. A Brahman of a high clan will marry ten, eleven, twenty, or even one hundred and fifty girls. He makes a business of it. He goes up and down the land marrying girls, receiving presents from their parents, and immediately thereafter bidding good-by to the brides; going home, he never returns to them. The illustrious Brahman need not bother himself with the care of supporting so many wives, for the parents pledge themselves to maintain the daughter all her life, if she stays with them a married virgin to the end. In case of such a marriage as this, the father is not required to spend money beyond his means, nor is it difficult for him to support the daughter, for she is useful to the family in doing the cooking and other household work; moreover, the father has the satisfaction first, of having given his daughter in marriage—and thereby having escaped disgrace and the ridicule of society; secondly, of having obtained for himself the bright mansions of the gods, since his daughter's husband is a Brahman of high clan.

But this form of polygamy does not exist among the Kshatriyas, because, as a member of the non-Brahman caste, a man is not allowed by religion, to beg or to receive gifts from others, except from friends; he therefore cannot support either many wives or many daughters. Caste and clan prejudice tyrannized the Rajputs of

North and Northwestern and Central India, who belong to the Kshatriyas or warrior caste, to such an extent that they were driven to introduce the inhuman and irreligious custom of female infanticide into their society. This cruel act was performed by the fathers themselves, or even by mothers, at the command of the husband whom they are bound to obey in all things.

It is a universal custom among the Rajputs for neighbors and friends to assemble to congratulate the father upon the birth of a child. If a boy is born, his birth is announced with music, glad songs and by distributing sweetmeats. If a daughter, the father coolly announces that "nothing" has been born into his family, by which expression it is understood that the child is a girl, and that she is very likely to be nothing in this world, and the friends go home grave and quiet.

After considering how many girls could safely be allowed to live, the father took good care to defend himself from caste and clan tyranny by killing the extra girls at birth, which was as easily

FAMINE CHILDREN, 1897

accomplished as destroying a mosquito or other annoying insect. Who can save a babe if the parents are determined to slay her, and eagerly watch for a suitable opportunity? Opium is generally used to keep the crying child quiet, and a small pill of this drug is sufficient to accomplish the cruel task; a skillful pressure upon the neck, which is known as the "putting nail to the throat," also answers the purpose. There are several other nameless methods that may be employed in sacrificing the innocents upon the unholy altar of the caste and clan system. Then there are not a few child-thieves who generally steal girls; even the wild animals are so intelligent and of such refined taste that they mock at British law, and almost always steal girls to satisfy their hunger.

Female infanticide, though not sanctioned by religion, and never looked upon as right by conscientious people, has, nevertheless, in those parts of India mentioned, been silently passed over unpunished by society in general.

As early as 1802 the British government enacted laws for the suppression of this horrid crime; and more than forty years ago Major Ludlow, a kind-hearted Englishman, induced the semi-independent States to prohibit this custom, which the Hindu princes did, by a mutual agreement not to allow any one to force the father of a girl to give more dowry than his circumstances should warrant, and to discourage extravagance in the celebration of marriages. But caste and clan prejudice could not be overcome so easily.

Large expenses might be stopped by law, but a belief, deeply rooted in the hearts and religiously observed by the people for centuries, could not be removed by external rules.

The Census of 1870 revealed the curious fact that three hundred children were stolen in one year by wolves from within the city of Umritzar, all the children being girls, and this under the very nose of the English government. In the year 1868 an English official, Mr. Hobart, made a tour of inspection through those parts of India where female infanticide was most practiced before the government enacted the prohibitory law.

As a result of careful observation, he came to the conclusion that this horrible practice was still followed in secret, and to an alarming extent.

The Census returns of 1880-81 show that there are fewer women than men in India by over five millions. Chief among the causes which have brought about this surprising numerical difference of the sexes may be named, after female infanticide in certain parts of the country, the imperfect treatment of the diseases of women in all parts of Hindustan, together with lack of proper hygienic care and medical attendance.

III

MARRIED LIFE

It is not easy to determine when the childhood of a Hindu girl ends and the married life begins. The early marriage system, although not the oldest custom of my country, is at least five hundred years older than the Christian era. According to Manu, eight years is the minimum, and twelve years of age the maximum marriageable age for a high caste girl.* The earlier the act of giving the daughter in marriage, the greater is the merit, for thereby the parents are entitled to rich rewards in heaven. There have always been exceptions to this rule, however. Among the eight kinds of marriages described in the law, there is one form that is

* A man aged thirty years shall marry a maiden of twelve who pleases him, or a man of twenty-four a girl of eight years of age.—*Manu* IX. 94.

only an agreement between the lovers to be loyal to each other; in this form of marriage there is no religious ceremony, nor even a third party to witness and confirm the agreement and relationship, and yet by the law this is regarded as completely lawful a marriage as any other. It is quite plain from this fact that all girls were not betrothed between the age of eight and twelve years, and also that marriage was not considered a religious institution by the Hindus in olden times. All castes and classes could marry in this form if they chose to do so. One of the most noticeable facts connected with this form is this: women as well as men were quite free to choose their own future spouses. In Europe and America women do choose their husbands, but it is considered a shame for a woman to be the first to request marriage, and both men and women will be shocked equally at such an occurrence; but in India, women had equal freedom with men, in this case at least. A woman might, without being put to shame, and without shocking the other party, come forward and select her own husband. The Svayamvara (selecting husband) was quite common until as late as the eleventh century, A. D., and even now, although very rarely, this custom is practiced by a few people.

I know of a woman in the Bombay presidency who is married to a Brahman according to this form. The first wife of the man is still living; the second wife, being of another caste, he could not openly acknowledge as his religiously wedded wife, but he could do so without going through the religious ceremony had she been of his own caste, as the act is sanctioned by Hindu law. The lawless behaviour of the Mahomedan intruders from the twelfth century, A. D., had much to do in universalizing infant marriage in India. A great many girls are given in marriage at the present day literally while they are still in their cradles; from five to eleven years is the usual period for their marriage among the Brahmans all over India. As it is absurd to assume that girls should be allowed to choose their future husbands in their infancy, this is done for them by their parents and guardians. In the northern part of the country the family barber is generally employed to select boys and girls to be married, it being considered too humiliating and mean an act on the part of parents and guardians to go out to seek their future daughters and sons-in-law.

Although Manu has distinctly said that twenty-four years is the minimum marriageable age for a young man, the popular custom defies the law. Boys of ten and twelve are now doomed to be married to girls of seven and eight years of age. A boy of a well-to-do family does not generally remain a bachelor after seventeen or eighteen years of age; the respectable but very poor families, even if they are of high caste, cannot afford to marry their boys so soon, but even among them it is a shame for a man to remain unmarried after twenty or twenty-five. Boys as well as girls have no voice in the selection of their spouses at the first marriage, but if a man lose his first wife, and marries a second time, *he* has a voice in the matter.

Although the ancient law-givers thought it desirable to marry girls when quite young, and consequently ignored their right to choose their own husbands, yet they were not altogether void of humane feelings. They have positively forbidden parents and guardians to give away girls in marriage unless good suitors were offered them.

> "To a distinguished, handsome suitor of equal caste should a father give his daughter in accordance with the prescribed rule, though she have not attained the proper age."—*Manu* IX. 88.
>
> "But the maiden, though marriageable, should rather stop in the father's house until death, than that he should ever give her to a man destitute of good qualities."—*Manu* IX. 89.

But, alas, here too the law is defied by cruel custom. It allows some men to remain unmarried, but woe to the maiden and to her family if she is so unfortunate as to remain single after the marriageable age. Although no law has ever said so, the popular belief is that a woman can have no salvation unless she be formally married. It is not, then, a matter of wonder that parents become extremely anxious when their daughters are over eight or nine and are unsought in marriage. Very few suitors offer to marry the daughters of poor parents, though they may be of high caste families. Wealth has its own pride and merit in India, as everywhere else in the world, but even this powerful wealth is as nothing before caste rule. A high caste man will never condescend to marry his daughter to a low caste man though he be a millionaire.

But wealth in one's own caste surpasses the merits of learning, beauty and honor; parents generally seek boys of well-to-do families for their sons-in-law. As the boys are too young to pass as possessing "good qualities," *i. e.*, learning, common-sense, ability to support and take care of a family, and respectable character, the parents wish to see their daughters safe in a family where she will, at least, have plenty to eat and to wear; they, of course, wish her to be happy with her husband, but in their judgment that is not the one thing needful. So long as they have fulfilled the custom, and thereby secured a good name in this world and heavenly reward in the next, their minds are not much troubled concerning the girl's fate. If the boy be of rich or middle class people, a handsome sum of money must be given to him and his family in order to secure the marriage; beside this, the girl's family must walk very humbly with this little god, for he is believed to be indwelt by the god Vishnu. Poor parents cannot have the advantage of marrying their daughters to boys of prosperous families, and as they must marry them to some one, it very frequently happens that girls of eight or nine are given to men of sixty and seventy, or to men utterly unworthy of the young maidens.

Parents who have the means to secure good-looking, prosperous men for their sons-in-law, take great care to consult the horoscopes of both parties in order to know the future of their daughters; in such cases, they are anxious to ascertain, over and above all things, that the girl shall not become a widow. If the daughter's horoscope reveals that her future husband is to survive her, the match is considered very satisfactory; but if it reveals the reverse, then a boy having a horoscope equally bad is sought for, because it is sincerely believed that in that case the guardian planets will wrestle with each other, and, as almost always happens, that the stronger, *i. e.*, the husband's planet will be victorious, or else both parties will fall in the conflict, and the husband and wife die together. A friend of mine informed me that three hundred horoscopes were rejected before one was found which agreed satisfactorily with her sister's guardian planet. Undoubtedly many suitors, who might make good husbands for these little girls, are for this reason rejected, and unworthy men fall to their lot; thus, the horoscope becomes a source of misery instead of blessing.

It not unfrequently happens that fathers give away their daughters in marriage to strangers without exercising care in making inquiry concerning the suitor's character and social position. It is enough to learn from the man's own statement, his caste and clan, and the locality of his home. I know of a most extraordinary marriage that took place in the following manner: the father was on a religious pilgrimage with his family, which consisted of his wife and two daughters, one nine and the other seven years of age, and they had stopped in a town to take rest for a day or two. One morning the father was bathing in the sacred river Godavari, near the town, when he saw a fine-looking man coming to bathe there also. After the ablution and the morning prayers were over, the father inquired of the stranger who he was and whence he came; on learning his caste, and clan, and dwelling-place, also that he was a widower, the father offered him his little daughter of nine, in marriage. All things were settled in an hour or so; next day the marriage was concluded, and the little girl placed in the possession of the stranger, who took her nearly nine hundred miles away from her home. The father left the place the day after the marriage without the daughter, and pursued his pilgrimage with a light heart; fortunately the little girl had fallen in good hands, and was well and tenderly cared for beyond all expectation, but the conduct of her father, who cared so little to ascertain his daughter's fate, is none the less censurable.

When the time to conclude the marriage ceremony draws near, the Hindu mother's affection for the girl frequently knows no bounds; she indulges her in endless ways, knowing that in a few days her darling will be torn away from her loving embrace. When she goes to pay the customary visit to her child's future mother-in-law many are the tearful entreaties and soul-stirring solicitations that she will be as kind and forbearing toward the little stranger as though she were her own daughter. The boy's mother is moved at this time, for she has a woman's heart, and she promises to be a mother to the little bride. On the day fixed for the marriage, parents formally give their daughters away to the boy; afterwards the young people are united by priests who utter the sacred texts and pronounce them man and wife in the presence of the sacred fire and of relatives and friends. The marriage being thus concluded, it is henceforth indissoluble.

> "Neither by sale nor by repudiation is a wife released from her husband; such we know the law to be which the Lord of creatures made of old."—*Manu* IX. 46.

Marriage is the only "Sacrament" administered to a high caste woman, accompanied with the utterance of the Vedic texts. It is to be presumed that the texts are introduced in honor of the man whom she marries, for no sacrament must be administered to him without the sacred formulæ. Henceforth the girl is his, not only his property, but also that of his nearest relatives.

> "For they (the ancient sages) declare that a bride is given to the family of her husband, and not to the husband alone."—*Apastamba* II. 10, 27, 3.

The girl now belongs to the husband's clan; she is known by his family name, and in some parts of India the husband's relatives will not allow her to be called by the first name that was given her by her parents; henceforth she is a kind of impersonal being. She can have no merit or quality of her own.

"Whatever be the qualities of the man with whom a woman is united in lawful marriage, such qualities even she assumes, like a river united with the ocean."—*Manu* IX. 22.

Many of our girls when asked in fun whether they would like soon to be married would innocently answer in the affirmative. They often see their sisters, cousins or playmates married; the occasion is one long to be remembered with pleasure. Even the poorest families take great pains to make it pleasant to everybody; children enjoy it most of all. There are gorgeous dresses, bright colored clothes, beautiful decorations, music, songs, fireworks, fun, plenty of fruit and sweet things to eat and to give away, lovely flowers, and the whole house is illuminated with many lamps. What can be more tempting to a child's mind than these? In addition to all this the big elephant is sometimes brought, on which the newly-married children ride in procession amidst all sorts of fun. Is it not grand enough for a child? Oh, I shall ride on the back of the elephant! thinks the girl; and there is something more besides; all the people in the house will wait on me, will make much of me; everybody will caress and try to please me. "Oh, what fun!"

"I like to have a cold, and be ill," said a girl of four. "Why, darling?" asked her mother, in surprise. "Oh, because," replied the little girl, "I like to eat my breakfast in bed, and then, too, everybody waits on me!"

Who has not heard remarks such as these, and laughed heartily over them? Children like even to be ill for the sake of being waited on. What wonder, then, if Hindu girls like being married for the sake of enjoying that much-coveted privilege! But little do these poor innocents know what comes after the fun. Little do they imagine that they must bid farewell to home and mother, to noisy merriment, and laughter, and to the free life of pure enjoyment. Sometimes the child desires to be married when, through superstition, she is ill-treated at home by her nearest relatives, otherwise there can be no reason except the enjoyment of fun that excites the desire in the girl's heart, for when the marriage takes place she is just emerging from babyhood.

Childhood is, indeed, the heyday of a Hindu woman's life. Free to go in and out where she pleases, never bothered by caste or other social restrictions, never worried by lesson-learning, sewing, mending or knitting, loved, petted and spoiled by parents, brothers and sisters, uncles and aunts, she is little different from a young colt whose days are spent in complete liberty. Then lo, all at once the ban of marriage is pronounced and the yoke put on her neck forever!

Immediately after the marriage ceremony is concluded the boy takes his girl-bride home and delivers her over to his own mother, who becomes from that time until the girl grows old enough to be given to her husband, her sole mistress, and who wields over the daughter-in-law undisputed authority!

It must be borne in mind that both in Northern and Southern India, the term "marriage" does not mean anything more than an irrevocable betrothal. The ceremony gone through at that time establishes religiously the conjugal relationship of both parties; there is a second ceremony that confirms the relationship both religiously and socially, which does not take place until the children attain the age of puberty. In Bengal the rule is somewhat different, and proves in many cases greatly injurious to the human system. In some very rare cases the girls are allowed to remain with their own parents for a time at least. In the North of India the little bride's lot is a happier one to begin with; she not being forced to go to her husband's home until she is about thirteen or fourteen years of age.

The joint family system, which is one of the peculiarities of Eastern countries, is very deeply rooted in the soil of India. There may not unfrequently be found four generations living under one roof. The house is divided into two distinct parts, namely, the outer and the inner court. The houses, as a rule, have but few windows, and they are usually dark; the men's court is comparatively light and good. Houses in country places are better than those in the crowded cities. Men and women have almost nothing in common.

The women's court is situated at the back of

the house, where darkness reigns perpetually. There the child-bride is brought to be forever confined. She does not enter her husband's house to be the head of a new home, but rather enters the house of the father-in-law to become the lowest of its members, and to occupy the humblest position in the family. Breaking the young bride's spirits is an essential part of the discipline of this new abode. She must never talk or laugh loudly, must never speak before or to the father and elder brother-in-law, or any other distant male relatives of her husband, unless commanded to do so. In Northern India, where all women wear veils, the young bride or woman covers her face with it, or runs into another room to show respect to them, when these persons enter an apartment where she happens to be. In Southern India, where women, as a rule, do not wear veils, they need not cover their faces; they rise to show respect to elders and to their husbands, and remain standing as long as they are obliged to be in their presence.

The mothers-in-law employ their daughters in

all kinds of household work, in order to give them a thorough knowledge of domestic duties. These children of nine or ten years of age find it irksome to work hard all day long without the hope of hearing a word of praise from the mother-in-law. As a rule, the little girl is scolded for every mistake she commits; if the work be well done, it is silently accepted, words of encouragement and praise from the elders being regarded as spoiling children and demoralizing them; the faults of the little ones are often mistaken for intentional offences, and then the artillery of abusive speech is opened upon them; thus, mortified and distressed, they seek to console themselves by shedding bitter tears in silence. In such sorrowful hours they miss the dear mother and her loving sympathy.

I must, however, do justice to the mothers-in-law. Many of them treat the young brides of their sons as their own children; many are kind and affectionate, but ignorant; they easily lose their temper and seem to be hard when they do not mean to be so. Others again, having themselves been the victims of merciless treatment in their childhood become hard-hearted; such an one will do all she can to torment the child by using abusive language, by beating her and slandering her before the neighbors. Often she is not satisfied by doing this herself, but induces and encourages the son to join her. I have several times seen young wives shamefully beaten by beastly young husbands who cherished no natural love for them.

As we have seen, the marriage is concluded without the consent of either party, and after it the bride is not allowed to speak or be acquainted with the husband until after the second ceremony, and even then the young couple must never betray any sign of their mutual attachment before a third party. Under such circumstances they seldom meet and talk; it may therefore be easily understood that being cut off from the chief means of forming attachment, the young couple are almost strangers, and in many cases do not like their relationship; and if in the midst of all this, the mother-in-law begins to encourage the young man to torment his wife in various ways, it is not strange that a feeling akin to hatred takes root between them. A child of thirteen was cruelly beaten by her husband in my presence for telling simple truth, that she did not like so well to be in his house as at her own home.

In spite, however, of all these drawbacks there is in India many a happy and loving couple that would be an honor to any nation. Where the conjugal relation is brightened by mutual love, the happy wife has nothing to complain of except the absence of freedom of thought and action; but since wives have never known from the beginning what freedom is, they are generally well content to remain in bondage; there is, however, no such thing as the family having pleasant times together.

Men spend their evenings and other leisure hours with friends of their own sex, either in the outer court or away from home. Children enjoy the company of father and mother alternately, by going in and out when they choose, but the children of young parents are never made happy by the father's caresses or any other demonstration of his love in the presence of the elders; the notion of false modesty prevents the young father from speaking to his children freely. The women of the family usually take their meals after the men have had theirs, and the wife, as a rule, eats what her lord may please to leave on his plate.

IV

WOMAN'S PLACE IN RELIGION AND SOCIETY

THE Hindu religion commands;

"Women must be honored and adorned by their fathers, brothers, husbands, and brothers-in-law, who desire their own welfare."

"Where women are honored, there the gods are pleased; but where they are not honored, no sacred rite yields rewards."

"Where the female relations live in grief, the family soon wholly perishes; but that family where they are not unhappy ever prospers."

"The houses on which female relations, not being duly honored, pronounce a curse, perish completely, as if destroyed by magic."

"Hence men who seek their own welfare, should always honor women on holidays and festivals with (gifts of) ornaments, clothes and dainty food."

"In that family where the husband is pleased with his wife, and the wife with her husband, happiness will assuredly be lasting."

"For if the wife is not radiant with beauty, she will

not attract her husband; but if she has no attractions for him, no children will be born."

"If the wife is radiant with beauty, the whole house is bright; but if she is destitute of beauty, all will appear dismal."—*Manu* III. 55-62.

These commandments are very significant. Our Aryan Hindus did, and still do honor woman to a certain extent. The honor bestowed upon the mother is without parallel in any other country. Although the woman is looked upon as an inferior being, the mother is nevertheless the chief person and worthy to receive all honor from the son. One of the great commandments of the Hindu Scriptures is, "Let thy mother be to thee like unto a god." *

Do not neglect what is useful.

* My readers would perhaps be interested to see these commandments; they are as follows:—" After having taught the Veda, the teacher instructs the pupil:

Say what is true.

Do thy duty.

Do not neglect the study of the Veda.

After having brought to thy teacher his proper reward, do not cut off the line of children! (*i. e.* Do not remain unmarried.)

Do not swerve from the truth.

Do not swerve from duty.

The mother is the queen of the son's household. She wields great power there, and is generally obeyed as the head of the family by her sons and by her daughters-in-law.

But there is a reverse side to the shield that should not be left unobserved. This is best studied in the laws of Manu, as all Hindus, with a few exceptions believe implicitly what that law-giver says about women:

> "It is the nature of women to seduce men in this world; for that reason the wise are never unguarded in the company of females."
>
> "For women are able to lead astray in this world not only a fool, but even a learned man, and to make him a slave of desire and anger."—*Manu* II. 213-214.

Do not neglect the learning and teaching of the Veda.
Do not neglect the sacrificial works due to the gods and fathers.
Let thy mother be to thee like unto a god.
Let thy father be to thee like unto a god.
Let thy teacher be to thee like unto a god.
Let thy guests be to thee like unto a god.
Whatever actions are blameless those should be regarded, not others.
Whatever good works have been performed by us, should be observed by thee, not others."—*Taittiriya Upanishad,* Valli, I. An. XI. 1, 2.

"Women do not care for beauty, nor is their attention fixed on age; thinking 'it is enough that he is a man,' they give themselves to the handsome and to the ugly."

"Through their passion for men, through their mutable temper, through their natural heartlessness, they become disloyal towards their husbands, however carefully they may be guarded in this world."

"Knowing their disposition, which the Lord of creatures laid in them at the creation, to be such, every man should most strenuously exert himself to guard them."

"When creating them, Manu allotted to women a love of their bed, of their seat and of ornament, impure desires, wrath, dishonesty, malice and bad conduct."

"For women no sacramental rite is performed with sacred texts, thus the law is settled; women who are destitute of strength and destitute of the knowledge of Vedic texts, are as impure as falsehood itself, that is a fixed rule."—*Manu* IX. 14-18.

Such is the opinion of Manu concerning all women; and all men with more or less faith in the law regard women, even though they be their own mothers, "as impure as falsehood itself."

"And to this effect many sacred texts are chanted also in the Vedas, in order to make fully known the true disposition of women; hear now those texts which refer to the expiation of their sins."

"'If my mother, going astray and unfaithful, conceived illicit desires, may my father keep that seed from me,' that is the scriptural text."—*Manu* IX. 19, 20.

Such distrust and such low estimate of woman's nature and character in general, is at the root of the custom of seclusion of women in India. This mischievous custom has greatly increased and has become intensely tyrannical since the Mahomedan invasion; but that it existed from about the sixth century, B.C., cannot be denied. All male relatives are commanded by the law to deprive the women of the household of all their freedom:—

"Day and night women must be kept in dependence by the males of their families, and if they attach themselves to sensual enjoyments, they must be kept under one's control."

"Her father protects her in childhood, her husband protects her in youth, and her sons protect her in old age; a woman is never fit for independence."—*Manu* IX. 2, 3.

"Women must particularly be guarded against evil inclinations, however trifling they may appear; for if they are not guarded, they will bring sorrow on two families."

"Considering that the highest duty of all castes, even weak husbands must strive to guard their wives."—*Manu* IX. 5, 6.

"No man can completely guard women by force; but they can be guarded by the employment of the following expedients:"

"Let the husband employ his wife in the collection and expenditure of his wealth, in keeping everything clean, in the fulfilment of religious duties, in the preparation of his food, and in looking after the household utensils."—*Manu* IX. 10, 11.

Those who diligently and impartially read Sanskrit literature in the original, cannot fail to recognize the law-giver Manu as one of those hundreds who have done their best to make woman a hateful being in the world's eye. To employ her in housekeeping and kindred occupations is thought to be the only means of keeping her out of mischief, the blessed enjoyment of literary culture being denied her. She is forbidden to read the sacred scriptures, she has no right to pronounce a single syllable out of them. To appease her uncultivated, low kind of desire by giving her ornaments to adorn her person, and by giving her dainty food together with an occasional bow which costs nothing, are the highest honors to which a Hindu woman is entitled. She, the loving mother of the nation, the devoted wife, the tender sister and affectionate daughter is never fit for independence, and is "as impure as falsehood itself." She is never to be trusted; matters of importance are never to be committed to her.

I can say honestly and truthfully, that I have never read any sacred book in Sanskrit literature without meeting this kind of hateful sentiment about women. True, they contain here and there a kind word about them, but such words seem to me a heartless mockery after having charged them, as a class, with crime and evil deeds.

Profane literature is by no means less severe or more respectful towards women. I quote from the ethical teachings, parts of a catechism and also a few proverbs:—

Q. What is cruel?
A. The heart of a viper.
Q. What is more cruel than that?
A. The heart of a woman.

Q. What is the cruelest of all?

A. The heart of a sonless, penniless widow.

A catechism on moral subjects written by a Hindu gentleman of high literary reputation says:—

Q. What is the chief gate to hell?

A. A woman.

Q. What bewitches like wine?

A. A woman.

Q. Who is the wisest of the wise?

A. He who has not been deceived by women who may be compared to malignant fiends.

Q. What are fetters to men?

A. Women.

Q. What is that which cannot be trusted?

A. Women.

Q. What poison is that which appears like nectar?

A. Women.

PROVERBS

"Never put your trust in women."

"Women's counsel leads to destruction."

"Woman is a great whirlpool of suspicion, a dwelling-place of vices, full of deceits, a hindrance in the way of heaven, the gate of hell."

Having fairly illustrated the popular belief about woman's nature, I now proceed to state woman's religion. Virtues such as truthfulness, forbearance, fortitude, purity of heart and uprightness, are common to men and women, but religion, as the word is commonly understood, has two distinct natures in the Hindu law; the masculine and the feminine. The masculine religion has its own peculiar duties, privileges and honors. The feminine religion also has its peculiarities.

The sum and substance of the latter may be given in a few words:—To look upon her husband as a god, to hope for salvation only through him, to be obedient to him in all things, never to covet independence, never to do anything but that which is approved by law and custom.

"Hear now the duties of women," says the law-giver, Manu:—

"By a girl, by a young woman, or even by an aged one, nothing must be done independently, even in her own house."

"In childhood, a female must be subject to her father, in youth, to her husband, when her lord is dead, to her sons; a woman must never be independent."

"She must not seek to separate herself from her father, husband, or sons; by leaving them she would make both her own and her husband's families contemptible."

"She must always be cheerful, clever in the management of her household affairs, careful in cleaning her utensils, and economical in expenditure."

"Him to whom her father may give her, or her brother with the father's permission, she shall obey as long as he lives, and when he is dead, she must not insult his memory."

"For the sake of procuring good fortune to brides, the recitation of benedictory texts, and the sacrifice to the Lord of creatures are used at weddings; but the betrothal by the father or guardian is the cause of the husband's dominion over his wife."

"The husband who wedded her with sacred texts, always gives happiness to his wife, both in season and out of season, in this world and in the next."

"Though destitute of virtue, or seeking pleasure elsewhere, or devoid of good qualities, yet a husband must be constantly worshipped as a god by a faithful wife."

"No sacrifice, no vow, no fast must be performed by women apart from their husbands; if a wife obeys her husband, she will for that reason alone, be exalted in heaven."

"A faithful wife, who desires to dwell after death with her husband, must never do anything that might displease him who took her hand whether he be alive or dead."—*Manu* V. 147-156.

"By violating her duty towards her husband, a wife is

disgraced in this world, after death she enters the womb of a jackal, and is tormented by diseases, the punishment of her sin."

"She who, controlling her thoughts, words and deeds, never slights her lord, resides after death with her husband in heaven, and is called a virtuous wife."

"In reward of such conduct, a female who controls her thoughts, speech and actions, gains in this life highest renown, and in the next world a place near her husband."—*Manu* V. 164-166.

MARITAL RIGHTS

"He only is a perfect man who consists of three persons united, his wife, himself and his offspring; thus says the Veda, and learned Brahmanas propound this maxim likewise, 'The husband is declared to be one with the wife.'"—*Manu* IX. 45.

The wife is declared to be the "marital property" of her husband, and is classed with "cows, mares, female camels, slave-girls, buffalo-cows, she-goats and ewes."—(See *Manu* IV. 48-51.)

The wife is punishable for treating her husband with aversion:—

"For one year let a husband bear with a wife who hates him; but after a lapse of a year, let him deprive her of her property and cease to live with her."

"She who shows disrespect to a husband who is addicted to some evil passion, is a drunkard, or diseased, shall be deserted for three months, and be deprived of her ornaments and furniture."—*Manu* IX. 77, 78.

"She who drinks spirituous liquor, is of bad conduct, rebellious, diseased, mischievous or wasteful, may at any time be superseded by another wife."

"A barren wife may be superseded in the eighth year, she whose children all die in the tenth, she who bears only daughters in the eleventh, but she who is quarrelsome without delay."—*Manu* IX. 80, 81.

"A wife who, being superseded, in anger departs from her husband's house, must either be instantly confined or cast off in the presence of the family."—*Manu* IX. 83.

"Though a man may have accepted a damsel in due form, he may abandon her if she be blemished or diseased, and if she have been given with fraud."—*Manu* IX. 72.

But no such provision is made for the woman; on the contrary, she must remain with and revere her husband as a god, even though he be "destitute of virtue, and seek pleasure elsewhere, or be devoid of good qualities, addicted to evil passion, fond of spirituous liquors or diseased," and what not!

How much impartial justice is shown in the treatment of womankind by Hindu law, can be fairly understood after reading the above quotations. In olden times these laws were enforced by the community; a husband had absolute power over his wife; she could do nothing but submit to his will without uttering a word of protest. Now, under the so-called Christian British rule, the woman is in no better condition than of old. True, the husband cannot as in the golden age, take her wherever she may be found, and drag her to his house, but his absolute power over her person has not suffered in the least. He is now bound to bring suit against her in the courts of justice to claim his "marital property," if she be unwilling to submit to him by any other means.

A near relative of mine had been given in her childhood in marriage to a boy whose parents agreed to let him stay and be educated with her in her own home. No sooner however, had the marriage ceremony been concluded than they forgot their agreement; the boy was taken to the home of his parents where he remained to grow up to be a worthless dunce, while his wife through the kindness and advanced views of her father, developed into a bright young woman and well accomplished.

Thirteen years later, the young man came to claim his wife, but the parents had no heart to send their darling daughter with a beggar who possessed neither the power nor the sense to make an honest living, and was unable to support and protect his wife. The wife too, had no wish to go with him since he was a stranger to her; under the circumstances she could neither love nor respect him. A number of orthodox people in the community who saw no reason why a wife should not follow her husband even though he be a worthless man, collected funds to enable him to sue her and her parents in the British Court of Justice. The case was examined with due ceremony and the verdict was given in the man's favor, according to Hindu law.* The wife was doomed to go with him. Fortunately she was

* In all cases except those directly connected with life and death, the British Government is bound according to the treaties concluded with the inhabitants of India, not to interfere with their social and religious customs and laws; judicial decisions are given accordingly.

soon released from this sorrowful world by cholera. Whatever may be said of the epidemics that yearly assail our country, they are not unwelcome among the unfortunate women who are thus persecuted by social, religious and State laws. Many women put an end to their earthly sufferings by committing suicide. Suits at law between husband and wife are remarkable for their rarity in the British Courts in India, owing to the ever submissive conduct of women who suffer silently, knowing that the gods and justice always favor the men.

The case of Rakhmabai, that has lately profoundly agitated Hindu society, is only one of thousands of the same class. The remarkable thing about her is that she is a well-educated lady, who was brought up under the loving care of her father, and had learned from him how to defend herself against the assaults of social and religious bigotries. But as soon as her father died the man who claimed to be her husband, brought suit against her in the court of Bombay. The young woman bravely defended herself, declining to go to live with the man on the ground that the marriage that was concluded without her consent could not be legally considered as such. Mr. Justice Pinhey, who tried the case in the first instance, had a sufficient sense of justice to refuse to force the lady to live with her husband against her will. Upon hearing this decision, the conservative party all over India rose as one man and girded their loins to denounce the helpless woman and her handful of friends. They encouraged the alleged husband to stand his ground firmly, threatening the British government with public displeasure if it failed to keep its agreement to force the woman to go to live with the husband according to Hindu law. Large sums were collected for the benefit of this man, Dadajee, to enable him to appeal against the decision to the full bench, whereupon, to the horror of all right-thinking people, the chief-justice sent back the case to the lower court for re-trial on its merits, as judged by the Hindu laws. The painful termination of this trial, I have in a letter written by my dear friend Rakhmabai herself, bearing date Bombay, March 18th, 1887. I quote from her letter:

"The learned and civilized judges of the full bench are determined to enforce, in this enlightened age, the inhuman laws enacted in barbaric times, four thousand years ago. They have not only commanded me to go to live with the man, but also have obliged me to pay the costs of the dispute. Just think of this extraordinary decision! Are we not living under the impartial British government, which boasts of giving equal justice to all, and are we not ruled by the Queen-Empress Victoria, herself a woman? My dear friend, I shall have been cast into the State prison when this letter reaches you; this is because I do not, and cannot obey the order of Mr. Justice Farran.

"There is no hope for women in India, whether they be under Hindu rule or British rule; some are of the opinion that my case so cruelly decided, may bring about a better condition for woman by turning public opinion in her favor, but I fear it will be otherwise. The hard-hearted mothers-in-law will now be greatly strengthened, and will induce their sons, who have for some reason or other, been slow to enforce the conjugal rights to sue their wives in the British Courts, since they are now fully assured that under no circumstances can the British government act adversely to the Hindu law."

Taught by the experience of the past, we are not at all surprised at this decision of the Bombay court. Our only wonder is that a defenseless woman like Rakhmabai dared to raise her voice in the face of the powerful Hindu law, the mighty British government, the one hundred and twenty-nine million men and the three hundred and thirty million gods of the Hindus, all these having conspired together to crush her into nothingness. We cannot blame the English government for not defending a helpless woman; it is only fulfilling its agreement made with the male population of India. How very true are the words of the Saviour, "Ye cannot serve God and Mammon." Should England serve God by protecting a helpless woman against the powers and principalities of ancient institutions, Mammon would surely be displeased, and British profit and rule in India might be endangered thereby. Let us wish it success, no matter if that success be achieved at the sacrifice of the rights and the comfort of over one hundred million women.

Meanwhile, we shall patiently await the advent of the kingdom of righteousness, wherein the weak, the lowly and the helpless shall be made happy because the great Judge Himself "shall wipe away all tears from their eyes."

V

WIDOWHOOD

We now come to the worst and most dreaded period of a high caste woman's life. Throughout India, widowhood is regarded as the punishment for a horrible crime or crimes committed by the woman in her former existence upon earth. The period of punishment may be greater or less, according to the nature of the crime. Disobedience and disloyalty to the husband, or murdering him in an earlier existence are the chief crimes punished in the present birth by widowhood.

If the widow be a mother of sons, she is not usually a pitiable object; although she is certainly looked upon as a sinner, yet social abuse and hatred are greatly diminished in virtue of the fact that she is a mother of the superior beings. Next in rank to her stands an ancient widow, because a virtuous, aged widow who has bravely withstood the thousand temptations and persecutions of her lot commands an involuntary respect from all people, to which may be added the honor given to old age quite independent of the individual. The widow-mother of girls is treated indifferently and sometimes with genuine hatred, especially so, when her daughters have not been given in marriage in her husband's life-time. But it is the child-widow or a childless young widow upon whom in an especial manner falls the abuse and hatred of the community as the greatest criminal upon whom Heaven's judgment has been pronounced.

In ancient times when the code of Manu was yet in the dark future and when the priesthood had not yet mutilated the original reading of a Vedic text concerning widows, a custom of remarriage was in existence.

Its history may be briefly stated:—The rite of child-marriage left many a girl a widow before she knew what marriage was, and her husband having died sonless had no right to enter into heaven and enjoy immortality, for "the father throws his debts on the son and obtains immortality if he sees the face of a living son. It is declared in the Vedas, endless are the worlds of those who have sons; there is no place for the man who is destitute of male offspring." The greatest curse that could be pronounced on enemies, was "may our enemies be destitute of offspring."

In order that these young husbands might attain the abodes of the blessed, the ancient sages invented the custom of "appointment" by which as among the Jews, the Hindu Aryans raised up seed for the deceased husband. The husband's brother, cousin or other kinsman successively was "appointed" and duly authorized to raise up offspring to the dead. The desired issue having been obtained any intercourse between the appointed persons was thenceforth considered illegal and sinful.

The woman still remained the widow of her deceased husband, and her children by the appointment were considered his heirs. Later on, this custom of "appointment" was gradually discouraged in spite of the Vedic text already quoted "there is no place for the man who is destitute of male offspring."

The duties of a widow are thus described in the code of Manu:—

"At her pleasure let her emaciate her body by living on pure flowers, roots and fruit; but she must never even mention the name of another man after her husband has died."

"Until death let her be patient of hardships, self-controlled, and chaste, and strive to fulfil that most excellent duty which is prescribed for wives who have one husband only."—*Manu* V. 157, 158.

". . . Nor is a second husband anywhere prescribed for virtuous women."—*Manu* V. 162.

"A virtuous wife who after the death of her husband constantly remains chaste, reaches heaven, . . ." —*Manu* V. 160.

"In reward of such conduct, a female who controls her thoughts, speech, and actions, gains in this life highest renown, and in the next world a place near her husband."*—*Manu* V. 166.

---

* It should be borne in mind that according to the popular belief there is no other heaven to a woman than the seat or mansion of her husband, where she shares the heavenly bliss with him in the next world if she

The following are the rules for a widower:—

"A twice-born man, versed in the sacred law, shall burn a wife of equal caste who conducts herself thus and dies before him, with the sacred fires used for the Agnihotra, and with the sacrificial implements."

"Having thus at the funeral, given the sacred fires to his wife who dies before him, he may marry again, and again kindle the (nuptial) fires."

"... And having taken a wife, he must dwell in his own house during the second period of his life."—*Manu* V. 167-169.

The self-immolation of widows on their deceased husband's pyre was evidently a custom invented by the priesthood after the code of Manu was compiled. The laws taught in the schools of Apastamba, Asvalayana and others older than Manu do not mention it, neither does the code of Manu. The code of Vishnu which is comparatively recent, says, that a woman "after the death of her husband should either lead a virtuous life or ascend the funeral pile of her husband."—*Vishnu* XXV. 2.

---

be faithful to him in thought, word and deed. The only place where she can be independent of him is in hell.

It is very difficult to ascertain the motives of those who invented the terrible custom of the so-called Suttee, which was regarded as a sublimely meritorious act. As Manu the greatest authority next to the Vedas did not sanction this sacrifice, the priests saw the necessity of producing some text which would overcome the natural fears of the widow as well as silence the critic who should refuse to allow such a horrid rite without strong authority. So the priests said there was a text in the Rig-veda which according to their own rendering reads thus:—

> "Om! let these women, not to be widowed, good wives, adorned with collyrium, holding clarified butter, consign themselves to the fire! Immortal, not childless, not husbandless, well adorned with gems, let them pass into the fire whose original element is water."

Here was an authority greater than that of Manu or of any other law giver, which could not be disobeyed. The priests and their allies, pictured heaven in the most beautiful colors and described various enjoyments so vividly that the poor widow became madly impatient to get to the blessed place in company with her departed husband. Not only was the woman assured of her getting into heaven by this sublime act, but also that by this great sacrifice she would secure salvation to herself and husband, and to their families to the seventh generation. Be they ever so sinful, they would surely attain the highest bliss in heaven, and prosperity on earth. Who would not sacrifice herself if she were sure of such a result to herself and her loved ones? Besides this, she was conscious of the miseries and degradation to which she would be subjected now that she had survived her husband. The momentary agony of suffocation in the flames was nothing compared to her lot as a widow. She gladly consented and voluntarily offered herself to please the gods and men. The rite of Suttee is thus described:—

"The widow bathed, put on new and bright garments, and, holding Kusha grass in her left hand, sipped water from her right palm, scattered some Tila grains, and then, looking eastward, quietly said, 'Om! on this day I, such and such a one, of such a family, die in the fire, that I may meet Arundhati, and reside in Svarga; that the years of my sojourn there may be as many as the hairs upon my husband, many scores multiplied; that I may enjoy with him the facilities of heaven, and bless my maternal and paternal ancestors, and those of my lord's line; that praised by Apsarasas, I may go far through the fourteen regions of Indra; that pardon may be given to my lord's sins whether he have ever killed a Brahman, broken the laws of gratitude and truth, or slain his friend. Now I do ascend this funeral pile of my husband, and I call upon you, guardians of the eight regions of the world, of sun, moon, air, of the fire, the ether, the earth, and the water, and my own soul. Yama, King of Death, and you, Day, Night and Twilight, witness that I die for my beloved, by his side upon his funeral pile.' Is it wonderful that the passage of the Sati to her couch of flame was like a public festival, that the sick and sorrowful prayed her to touch them with her little, fearless, conquering hand, that criminals were let loose if she looked upon them, that the horse which carried her was never used again for earthly service?" (E. Arnold.)

The act was supposed to be altogether a voluntary one, and no doubt it was so in many cases. Some died for the love stronger than death which they cherished for their husbands. Some died not because they had been happy in this world, but because they believed with all the heart that they should be made happy hereafter. Some to obtain great renown, for tombstones and monuments were erected to those who thus died, and afterwards the names were inscribed on the long list of family gods; others again, to escape the thousand temptations, and sins and miseries which they knew would fall to their lot as widows. Those who from pure ambition or from momentary impulse, declared their intentions thus to die, very often shrank from the fearful altar; no sooner did they feel the heat of the flames than they tried to leap down and escape the terrible fate; but it was too late. They had taken the solemn oath which must never be broken, priests and other men were at hand to force them to remount the pyre. In Bengal, where this custom was most in practice, countless, fearful tragedies of this description occurred even after British rule was long established there. Christian missionaries petitioned the government to abolish this inhuman custom, but they were told that the social and religious customs of the people constituted no part of the business of the government, and that their rule in India might be endangered by such interference. The custom went on unmolested until the first quarter of the present century, when a man from among the Hindus, Raja Ram Mohun Roy, set his face against it, and declared that it was not sanctioned by the Veda as the priests claimed. He wrote many books on this subject, showing the wickedness of the act, and with the noble co-operation of a few friends, he succeeded at last in getting the government to abolish it. Lord William Bentinck, when Governor-general of India, had the moral courage to enact the famous law of 1829, prohibiting the Suttee rite within British domains, and holding as criminals, subject to capital punishment, those who countenanced it. But it was not until 1844 that the law had any effect upon orthodox Hindu minds.

That the text quoted from the Veda was mistranslated, and a part of it forged, could have been easily shown had all Brahmans known the meaning of the Veda. The Vedic language is the oldest form of Sanskrit, and greatly differs from the later form. Many know the Vedas by heart and repeat them without a mistake, but few indeed, are those that know the meaning of the texts they repeat. "The Rig-veda," says Max Müller, "so far from enforcing the burning of widows, shows clearly that this custom was not sanctioned during the earliest period of Indian history. According to the hymns of the Rig-veda, and the Vedic ceremonial contained in the Grihya-sutras, the wife accompanies the corpse of her husband to the funeral pile, but she is there addressed with a verse taken from the Rig-veda, and ordered to leave her husband and to return to the world of the living."

"'Rise, woman,' it is said, 'come to the world of life, thou sleepest nigh unto him whose life is gone. Come to us. Thou hast thus fulfilled the duties of a wife to the husband, who once took thy hand and made thee a mother.'"

"This verse is preceded by the very verse which the later Brahmans have falsified and quoted in support of their cruel tenet. The reading of the verse is beyond all doubt, for there is no various reading, in our sense of the word, in the whole of Rig-veda. Besides, we have the commentaries and the ceremonials, and nowhere is there any difference to the text or its meaning. It is addressed to the other women who are present at the funeral, and who have to pour oil and butter on the pile.

"'May these women who are not widows, but have good husbands, draw near with oil and butter. These who are mothers may go up first to the altar, without tears, without sorrow, but decked with fine jewels.'"

It was by falsifying a single syllable that the unscrupulous priests managed to change entirely the meaning of the whole verse. Those who know the Sanskrit characters can easily understand that the falsification very likely originated in the carelessness of the transcriber or copyist, but for all that the priests who permitted the error are not excusable in the least. Instead of comparing the verse with its context, they translated it as their fancy dictated and thus under the pretext of religion they have been the cause of destroying countless lives for more than two thousand years.

Now that the Suttee-rite, partly by the will of the people and partly by the law of the empire, is prohibited, many good people feel easy in their minds, thinking that the Hindu widow has been delivered from the hand of her terrible fate; but little do they realize the true state of affairs!

Throughout India, except in the Northwestern Provinces, women are put to the severest trial imaginable after the husband's death. The manner in which they are brought up and treated from their earliest childhood compels them to be slaves to their own petty little interests, to be passionate lovers of ornaments and of self-adornment, but no sooner does the husband die than they are deprived of every gold and silver ornament, of the bright-colored garments, and of all the things they love to have about or on their persons. The cruelty of social customs does not stop here. Among the Brahmans of Deccan the heads of all widows must be shaved regularly every fortnight. Some of the lower castes, too, have adopted this custom of shaving widows' heads, and have much pride in imitating their high-caste brethren. What woman is there who does not love the wealth of soft and glossy hair with which nature has so generously decorated her head? A Hindu woman thinks it worse than death to lose her beautiful hair. Girls of fourteen and fifteen who hardly know the reason why they are so cruelly deprived of everything they like, are often seen wearing sad countenances, their eyes swollen from shedding bitter tears. They are glad to find a dark corner where they may hide their faces as if they had done something shameful and criminal. The widow must wear a single coarse garment, white, red or brown. She must eat only one meal during the twenty-four hours of a day. She must never take part in family feasts and jubilees, with others. She must not show herself to people on auspicious occasions. A man or woman thinks it unlucky to behold a widow's face before seeing any other object in the morning. A man will postpone his journey if his path happens to be crossed by a widow at the time of his departure.

A widow is called an "inauspicious" thing.

The name "rand," by which she is generally known, is the same that is borne by a Nautch girl or a harlot. The relatives and neighbors of the young widow's husband are always ready to call her bad names, and to address her in abusive language at every opportunity. There is scarcely a day of her life on which she is not cursed by these people as the cause of their beloved friend's death. The mother-in-law gives vent to her grief by using such language as, when once heard, burns into a human heart. In short, the young widow's life is rendered intolerable in every possible way. There may be exceptions to this rule, but, unhappily, they are not many. In addition to all this, the young widow is always looked upon with suspicion, and closely guarded as if she were a prisoner, for fear she may at any time bring disgrace upon the family by committing some improper act. The purpose of disfiguring her by shaving her head, by not allowing her to put ornaments or bright, beautiful garments on her person, is to render her less attractive to a man's eye. Not allowing her to eat more than once a day, and compelling her to abstain from food altogether on sacred days, is a part of the discipline by which to mortify her youthful nature and desire. She is closely confined to the house, forbidden even to associate with her female friends as often as she wishes; no man except her father, brother, uncles and her aunt-cousins (who are regarded as brothers) are allowed to see or speak with her. Her life then, destitute as it is of the least literary knowledge, void of all hope, empty of every pleasure and social advantage, becomes intolerable, a curse to herself and to society at large. She has but few persons to sympathize with her. Her own parents, with whom she lives in case her husband has no relatives, or if his relatives are unable to take care of her, do, of course, sympathize with her, but custom and religious faith have a stronger hold upon them than parental love. They, too, regard their daughter with concern, lest she bring disgrace upon their family.

It is not an uncommon thing for a young widow without occupation that may satisfy mind and heart, and unable longer to endure the slights and suspicions to which she is perpetually subjected, to escape from her prison-home. But when she gets away from it, where shall she go? No respectable family, even of a lower caste, will have her for a servant. She is completely ignorant of any art by which she may make an honest living. She has nothing but the single garment which she wears on her person. Starvation and death stare her in the face; no ray of hope penetrates her densely-darkened mind. What can she do? The only alternative before her is either to commit suicide or, worse still, accept a life of infamy and shame. Oh, cruel, cruel is the custom that drives thousands of young widows to such a fate. Here is a prayer by a woman doomed to life-long misery, which will describe her own and her sisters' feelings better than any words of mine. It was written by a pupil of a British Zenana missionary, one of the few Hindu women who can read and write, and one who has tasted the bitter sorrows and degradation of Hindu widowhood from her childhood,—

"Oh Lord, hear my prayer! No one has turned an eye on the oppression that we poor women suffer, though with weeping, and crying and desire, we have turned to all sides, hoping that some one would save us. No one has lifted up his eyelids to look upon us, nor inquire into our case. We have searched above and below, but Thou art the only One who wilt hear our complaint,—Thou knowest our impotence, our degradation, our dishonor.

"O Lord, inquire into our case. For ages dark ignorance has brooded over our minds and spirits; like a cloud of dust it rises and wraps us round, and we are like prisoners in an old and mouldering house, choked and buried in the dust of custom, and we have no strength to go out. Bruised and beaten, we are like the dry husks of the sugar-cane when the sweet juice has been extracted. All-knowing God, hear our prayer! forgive our sins and give us power of escape, that we may see something of Thy world. O Father, when shall we be set free from this jail? For what sin have we been born to live in this prison? From Thy throne of judgment justice flows, but it does not reach us; in this, our life-long misery, only injustice comes near us.

"Thou hearer of prayer, if we have sinned against Thee, forgive, but we are too ignorant to know what sin is. Must the punishment of sin fall on those who are too ignorant to know what it is? O great Lord, our name is written with drunkards, with lunatics, with imbeciles, with the very animals; as they are not responsible, we are not. Criminals, confined in the jails for life, are happier than we, for they know something of Thy world. They were not born in prison, but we have not for one day, no, not even in our dreams, seen Thy world; to us it is nothing but a name; and not having seen the world, we cannot know Thee, its maker. Those who have seen Thy works may learn to understand Thee, but for us, who are shut in, it is not possible to learn to know Thee. We see only the four walls of the house. Shall we call them the world, or India? We have been born in this jail, we have died here, and are dying.

"O Father of the world, hast Thou not created us? Or has perchance, some other god made us? Dost Thou care only for men? Hast Thou no thought for us women? Why hast Thou created us male and female? O Almighty, hast Thou not power to make us other than we are, that we too might have some share in the comforts of this life? The cry of the oppressed is heard even in the world. Then canst Thou look upon our victim hosts, and shut Thy doors of justice? O God Almighty and Unapproachable, think upon Thy mercy, which is a vast sea, and remember us. O Lord, save us, for we cannot bear our hard lot; many of us have killed ourselves, and we are still killing ourselves. O God of mercy, our prayer to Thee is this, that the curse may be removed from the women of India. Create in the hearts of the men some sympathy, that our lives may no longer be passed in vain longing, that saved by Thy mercy, we may taste something of the joys of life."

A Hindu gentleman contributes an article entitled "The Hindu Widow," to "The Nineteenth Century." I quote from this as testimony from the other sex, of the truthfulness of my statement, lest I should appear to exaggerate the miserable condition to which my sister-widows are doomed for life:—

"The widow who has no parents has to pass her whole life under the roof of her father-in-law, and then she knows no comfort whatever. She has to meet from her late husband's relations only unkind looks and unjust reproaches. She has to work like a slave, and for the reward of all her drudgery she only receives hatred and abhorrence from her mother-in-law and sisters-in-law. If there is any disorder in the domestic arrangements of the family the widow is blamed and cursed for it. Among Hindus, women cannot inherit any paternal property, and if a widow is left any property by her husband she cannot call it her own. All her wealth belongs to her son, if she has any, and if she has nobody to inherit it she is made to adopt an heir, and give him all her property directly he comes of age, and herself live on a bare allowance granted by him. Even death cannot save a widow from indignities. For when a wife dies she is burnt in the clothes she had on, but a widow's corpse is covered with a coarse white cloth, and there is little ceremony at her funeral. . . .

"'The English have abolished Sati (Suttee), but alas! neither the English nor the angels know what goes on in our houses, and the Hindus not only do not care, but think it good!' Such were the words of a widow; and well might she exclaim that 'neither the English nor the angels know, and that the Hindus not only don't care, but think it good;' for Hindu as I am, I can vouch for her statement that very few Hindus have a fair knowledge of the actual sufferings of the widows among them, and fewer still care to know the evils and horrors of the barbarous custom which victimizes their own sisters and daughters in so ruthless a manner; nay, on the contrary, the majority of the orthodox Hindus consider the practice to be good and salutary. Only the Hindu widows know their own sufferings; it is perfectly impossible for any other mortal, or even 'the angels,' (as the widow says), to realize them. One can easily imagine how hard the widow's lot must be. . . . when to the continuous course of fastings, self-inflictions and humiliations is added the galling ill-treatment which she receives from her own relations and friends. To a Hindu widow death is a thousand times more welcome than her miserable existence. It is no doubt this feeling that drove in former times many widows to immolate themselves on the funeral pyres of their dead husbands."—DEVENDRA N. DAS, *Nineteenth Century, September*, 1886.

There is a class of reformers who think that they will meet all the wants of widows by establishing the re-marriage system. This system should certainly be introduced for the benefit of the infant widows who wish to marry on coming to age; but at the same time it should be remembered that this alone is incapable and insufficient to meet their wants.

In the first place, widow-marriage among the high-caste people will not for a long time become an approved custom. The old idea is too deeply rooted in the heart of society to be soon removed. Secondly, there are not many men who will boldly come forward and marry widows, even if the widows wish it. It is one thing to talk about doing things contrary to the approved custom, but to practice is quite another matter. It is now about fifty years since the movement called widow-marriage among the high-caste Hindus was started, but those who have practiced it are but few. I have known men of great learning and high reputation who took oaths to the effect that if they were to become widowers and wished to marry again they would marry widows. But no sooner had their first wives died than they forgot all about the oaths and married pretty little maidens. Society threatens them with excommunication, their friends and relatives entreat them with tears in their eyes, others offer money and maids if they will consent to give up the idea of marrying a widow. Can flesh and blood resist these temptations? If some men wish to be true to their convictions, they must be prepared to suffer perpetual martyrdom. After marrying a widow they are sure to be cut off from all connection with society and friends, and even with their nearest relatives. In such a case no faithful Hindu would ever give them assistance if they were to fall in distress or become unable to earn their daily bread; they will be ridiculed by, and hated of all men. How many people are there in the world who would make this tremendous sacrifice on the altar of conscience? The persecution to be endured by people who transgress established customs is so great that life becomes a burden. A few years ago a high-caste man in

Cutch, (Northwestern India,) ventured to marry a widow, but to endure the persecution which ensued, was beyond his power, and the wretched fellow was soon after found dead, having committed suicide.

Re-marriage, therefore, is not available, nor would it be at all times desirable, as a mitigation of the sufferer's lot. So the poor, helpless high-caste widow with the one chance of ending her miseries in the Suttee rite taken away from her, remains as in ages past with none to help her.

VI

HOW THE CONDITION OF WOMEN TELLS UPON SOCIETY

THOSE who have done their best to keep women in a state of complete dependence and ignorance, vehemently deny that this has anything to do with the present degradation of the Hindu nation. I pass over the hundreds of nonsenses which are brought forward as the strongest reasons for keeping women in ignorance and dependence. They have already been forced out into the broad day-light of a generous civilization, and have been put to the fiery proof of science and found wanting. Above all, the noble example of thousands of women in many countries have burned the so-called reasons to ashes. But their ghosts are still hovering over the land of the Hindus and are frightening the timid and the ignorant to death. Let us hope that in God's good time, all these devils shall be forever cast out of India's body; meanwhile it is our duty to take the matter into serious consideration, and to put forth our best endeavors to hasten the glad day for India's daughters, aye, and for her sons also; because in spite of the proud assertions of our brethren that they have not suffered from the degradation of women, their own condition betrays but too plainly the contrary.

Since men and women are indissolubly united by Providence as members of the same body of human society, each must suffer when their fellow-members suffer, whether they will confess it or not. In the animal as well as in the vegetable kingdom, nature demands that all living beings shall freely comply with its conditions of growth or they cannot become that which they were originally designed to be. Why should any exception to this law be made for the purdah women? Closely confined to the four walls of their house, deprived throughout their lives of the opportunity to breathe healthy fresh air, or to drink in the wholesome sunshine, they become weaker and weaker from generation to generation, their physical statures dwarfed, their spirits crushed under the weight of social prejudices and superstitions, and their minds starved from absolute lack of literary food and of opportunity to observe the world. Thus fettered, in ninety cases out of a hundred, at the least calculation, they grow to be selfish slaves to their petty individual interests, indifferent to the welfare of their own immediate neighbors, much more to their nation's well-being. How could these imprisoned mothers be expected to bring forth children better than themselves, for as the tree and soil are, so shall the fruit be. Consequently we see all around us in India a generation of men least deserving that exalted appellation.

The doctrine of "pre-natal influence" can nowhere be more satisfactorily proved than in India. The mother's spirits being depressed, and mind as well as body weakened by the monotony and inactivity of her life, the unborn child cannot escape the evil consequences. The men of Hindustan do not when babes, suck from the mother's breast true patriotism, and in their boyhood, the mother, poor woman, is unable to develope that divine faculty in them owing to her utter ignorance of the past and present condition of her native land. Fault-finding with neighbors, bitter feelings towards tyrant relatives expressed in words and actions, selfish interest in personal and family affairs, these are the chief lessons that children learn at the mother's knee, from babyhood up to the seventh or eighth year of age.

Again, how does it come to pass that each succeeding generation grows weaker than the one preceding it, if not because the progenitors of each generation lack the mental and physical strength which children are destined to inherit? The father may have been free and healthy in mind, as well as in body, but the mother was not; she undoubtedly has bequeathed the fatal legacy of weakness and dullness to her children. The complete submission of women under the Hindu law has in the lapse of millenniums of years converted them into slavery-loving creatures. They are glad to lean upon any one and be altogether dependent, and thus it has come to pass that their sons as a race, desire to depend upon some other nation, and not upon themselves. The seclusion, complete dependence and the absolute ignorance forced upon the mothers of our nation have been gradually and fatally telling upon the mental and physical health of the men, and in these last times they have borne the poisonous fruit that will compel the Hindu nation to die a miserable and prolonged death if a timely remedy is not taken to them.

Moreover the Hindu woman's ignorance prevents liberal-minded and progressive men from making necessary and important changes in the manners and habits of the household; bigoted women also prevent their husbands and sons from such important enterprises as crossing the ocean in the pursuit of useful knowledge, or for purposes of trade.

To add to all the disabilities of the Hindu mother in the discharge of her sacred maternal duties, she is as a rule, wholly ignorant of the commonest hygienic laws. It must be remembered that she is herself a girl scarcely out of her babyhood, when she becomes a mother. At about fourteen, fifteen or sixteen years of age she cannot be expected to know all that is necessary in order to take good care of her child. The first and second of the children of this young mother usually die, and if they survive, they are apt to grow up to be weak and unhealthy adults. Until they are seven or eight years of age, the children of the household are left to themselves without any one to take care of them, and no influence is exerted to mould their character at this most interesting and important period of life. Who but an intelligent and loving mother can do this all-important work for her children at that age?

Having thus far endeavored to bring to the notice of Western women the condition of a class of their oriental sisters, I now desire to direct their attention definitely to our chief needs. After many years of careful observation and thought, I have come to the conclusion that the chief needs of high-caste Hindu women are:—1st, Self-Reliance; 2nd, Education; 3rd, Native Women Teachers.

I. Self-Reliance.—The state of complete dependence in which men are required by the law-giver to keep women from birth to the end of their lives makes it impossible for them to have self-reliance, without which a human being becomes a pitiful parasite. Women of the working classes are better off than their sisters of high castes in India, for in many cases they are obliged to depend upon themselves, and an opportunity for cultivating self-reliance is thus afforded them by which they largely profit. But high-caste women, unless their families are actually destitute of means to keep them, are shut up within the four walls of their house. In aftertime, if they are left without a protector, *i. e.*, a male relative to support and care for them, they literally do not know what to do with themselves. They have been so cruelly cropped in their early days that self-reliance and energy are dead within them; helpless victims of indolence and false timidity they are easily frightened out of their wits and have little or no strength to withstand the trials and difficulties which must be encountered by a person on her way toward progress. But it is idle to hope that the condition of my country-women will ever improve without individual self-reliance; therefore, is it not the duty of our Western sisters to teach them how they may become self-reliant?

II. Education.—The lack of education among the women of India can be fairly realized by scanning the report of the Educational Commission for 1883, and the census returns of 1880-81. Of the ninety-nine million seven hundred thousand women and girls directly under British rule, ninety-nine and one-half millions are returned as unable to read and write; the remaining two hundred thousand who are able either to read or write, cannot all be reckoned as educated, for the school-going period of a girl is generally between seven and nine years of age; within that short time she acquires little more than ability to read the second or the third vernacular reading-book, and a little knowledge of arithmetic which usually comprehends no more than the four simple rules. It should be remembered that the two hundred thousand women able to read or write are the "alumnæ" of the government schools, mission schools, private schools conducted by the inhabitants of India independently, private societies and Zenana mission agencies all reckoned together. It is surprising how even this small number of women can have acquired the limited knowledge indicated, when we consider the powers and principalities that are incessantly fighting against female education in India. Girls of nine and ten when recently out of school and given in marriage are wholly cut off from reading or writing, because it is a shame for a young woman or girl to hold a paper or book in her hand, or to read in the presence of others in her husband's house. It is a popular belief among high-caste women that their husbands will die if they should read or should hold a pen in their fingers. The fear of becoming a widow overcomes their hunger and thirst for knowledge. Moreover the little wives can get but scanty time to devote to self-culture; any one fortunate enough to possess the desire and able to command the time is in constant fear of being seen by her husband's relatives. Her employment cannot long be kept secret where every one is on the lookout, and when discovered she is ridiculed, laughed at and even commanded by the elders to leave off this nonsense. Her literary pursuits are now at an end unless the proceedings of the elders be interfered with by her progressive husband; but alas, such husbands are extremely rare. Our schools, too, are not very attractive to children; the teachers of primary schools, (and it is to these schools that girls are usually sent), are but nominally educated, and do not know how to make the lessons interesting for children. Consequently a great many of the girls who have been educated up to the second or third standard (grade) in these primary schools make it their business quickly to forget their lessons as soon as they find an opportunity. Shut in from the world and destitute of the ability to engage in newspaper and useful book-reading, they have little or no knowledge of common things around them, and of the most important events that are daily occurring in their own or foreign lands. Ignorant, unpatriotic, selfish and uncultivated, they drag the men down with them into the dark abyss where they dwell together without hope, without ambition to be something or to do something in the world.

III. Native Women Teachers.—American and English women as Zenana missionaries are doing all they can to elevate and enlighten India's daughters. These good people deserve respect and praise from all, and the heart-felt thanks of those for whose elevation they toil, but the disabilities of an unfriendly climate, and of an unknown tongue make it exceedingly difficult for them to enter upon their work for some time after reaching India; and then, "what are these among so many?" They are literally lost among the nearly one hundred millions of women under British rule to whom must be added several millions more under Hindu and Mahommedan rule. In America and in England we hear encouraging reports from mission fields, which state that a few thousand Hindu and Mahommedan women and girls are being instructed in schools or in their own homes, but these seem as nothing, compared to the vast multitude of the female population of Hindustan. In a country where castes and the seclusion of women are regarded as essential tenets of the national creed, we can scarcely hope for a general spread of useful knowledge among women, through either men of their own race or through foreign women. All experience in the past history of mankind has shown that efforts for the elevation of a nation must come from within and work outward to be effectual.

The one thing needful, therefore, for the general diffusion of education among women in India is a body of persons from among themselves who shall make it their life-work to teach by precept and example their fellow-countrywomen.

VII

THE APPEAL

IN the preceding chapters I have tried to tell my readers briefly the sad story of my countrywomen, and also to bring to their notice what are our chief needs. We, the women of India, are hungering and thirsting for knowledge; only education under God's grace, can give us the needful strength to rise up from our degraded condition.

Our most pressing want and one which must immediately be met is women-teachers of our own nationality. How can these women-teachers be supplied? I have long been thinking over this matter and now I am prepared to give answer.

Among the inhabitants of India, the high-caste people rank as the most intelligent; they have been a refined and cultivated race for more than two thousand years. The women of these castes have been and still are kept in ignorance, yet they have inherited from their fathers to a certain degree, quickness of perception and intelligence. A little care and judicious education bestowed upon them will make many of them competent teachers and able workers. That this statement is not altogether visionary on my part, has been proven by the gratifying results of careful training in the person of Chandramukhi Bose, M. A., now lady principal of Bethune School, Calcutta, Kadambini B. Ganguli, B. A., M. B., and also others who have successfully passed their examinations in the Calcutta University. The professors of the Woman's Medical College of Pennsylvania will bear testimony to the ability of the late Dr. Anandibai Joshee. Had her life been spared a little longer she would have shown to the world that the Hindu woman, in spite of all drawbacks equals any woman of civilized countries.

Again, according to the census of 1881 there

were in India twenty million nine hundred and thirty thousand six hundred and twenty-six widows, of all ages and castes. Among these were six hundred and sixty-nine thousand one hundred widows under nineteen years of age, viz.:

Under nine years of age............	78,976	
From ten to fourteen years of age....	207,388	
From fifteen to nineteen years of age..	382,736	
		669,100

Girls of nine and ten, or thirteen years of age, whose betrothed husbands are dead, are virgin widows, and these, if of high-caste families, must remain single throughout life. Now if there were suitable educational institutions where young widows who might wish to be independent of their relatives and make an honest living for themselves, might go to be instructed in useful handiwork, and educated for teachers, many horrid occurrences might be prevented, and at the same times these widows would prove a welcome blessing to their countrywomen. But alas! institutions have not been found anywhere in

India where high-caste widows can receive shelter and education.

In the year 1866, an eminent English lady, Miss Mary Carpenter, made a short tour in India, with a view to find some way by which women's condition in that country might be improved. She at once discovered that the chief means by which the desired end might be accomplished was by furnishing women-teachers for the Hindu zenanas. She suggested that the British government should establish normal schools for training women-teachers and that scholarships should be awarded to girls in order to prolong their school-going period, and to assist indigent women, who would otherwise be unable to pursue their studies. In response to Miss Carpenter's appeal upon her return to England, the British government founded several schools for women in India, and in honor of this good lady a few "Mary Carpenter scholarships" were endowed by benevolent persons. These schools which I have personally inspected, were opened to women of every caste, and while they have undoubtedly been of use, they have not realized the hopes of their founder, partly because of the impossibility of keeping caste-rules in them, and partly on account of the inadequacy of the arrangements for attendance. When a high-caste widow takes it upon herself to go to school, she cannot hope, except in cases which are extremely rare, to receive any kind of help from her own relatives; so she is thrown out a penniless, helpless, forlorn creature to face the world alone. If then she is so fortunate as to be sheltered in a normal school and is awarded a studentship she finds this scarcely enough to keep her from starvation, its money value being from twelve to twenty or twenty-five dollars per year; but she cannot get even this scanty support from the educational department, unless she pass a certain examination. How can an illiterate widow hope to pass that examination?

Besides these government normal schools for women, of which at the present time, there are probably six throughout all India, there are a few foreign mission schools where a woman may find shelter and instruction, but if she be an orthodox Hindu by faith, and of a respectable family, she will on no account take refuge with people of a strange religion and country. There are exceptions of course to this statement, but as a rule, a high-caste Hindu woman prefers death to this alternative. She knows that if she goes to live with missionaries she must lose caste, and that she must study their Bible, and perhaps in the end be induced to forsake her ancestral faith and embrace a strange one. No woman of any religion in which she firmly believes whether it appear to others to be true or false, would violate her conscience simply for food and shelter. That the fear of being tempted to abjure one's religion for the sake of worldly gain should prevent many an excellent Hindu widow from going to foreign missionary schools is undoubted. She honestly believes that if her life is rendered intolerable by domestic misery she can drown herself in some sacred river by which deed she will not only escape the wretchedness of this life, but her past sins will be forgiven, and a place in heaven se-

SHÂRADÂ SADAN BUNGALOW AT POONA

cured, but to forsake her ancestral religion under any circumstances would doom her to eternal perdition in the world to come.

Is there then no way of helping and educating these high-caste widows? Can none of these obstacles be removed from her path? Yes! they can be removed, and the course which in my judgment can most advantageously be taken in order to succor the widows and the women of India in general, may be stated as follows:—

I. Houses should be opened for the young and high-caste child-widows where they can take shelter without the fear of losing their caste, or of being disturbed in their religious belief and where they may have entire freedom of action as relates to caste-rules, such as cooking of food, etc., provided they do not violate the rules or disturb the peace of the house wherein they have taken up their abode.

II. In order to help them make an honorable and independent living, they should be taught in these houses to be teachers, governesses, nurses and housekeepers, and should become skilled in other forms of hand-work, according to their taste and capacity.

III. These houses should be under the superintendence and management of influential Hindu ladies and gentlemen, who should be pledged to make each house a happy home and an instructive institution for those who seek its opportunities.

IV. The services of well-qualified American ladies as assistants and teachers should be secured in order to afford the occupants of the houses the combined advantage of Eastern and Western civilization and education.

V. Libraries containing the best books on history, science, art, religions and other departments of literature should be established in these houses for the benefit of their inmates and of other women in their vicinity who may wish to read. Lectureships should also be established in the libraries, and the lecturers should be engaged with the distinct understanding that they do not speak irreverently of any religion or sacred custom while lecturing in that house or library; the lecturers should embrace in their topics, hygiene, geography, elementary science, foreign travel, etc., and the lectures should be designed primarily to open the eyes and ears of those who long have dwelt in the prison-house of ignorance, knowing literally nothing of God's beautiful world.

It is my intention after my return home (which I trust may be within a year from this time) to establish at least one such institution. I am fully aware of the great responsibility the trial—and it may be the failure—will involve; but as some one must make a beginning, I am resolved to try, trusting that God, who knows the need of my countrywomen, will raise up able workers to forward this cause, whether I succeed in it or not. The great majority of my country-people being most bitterly opposed to the education of women, there is little hope of my getting from them either good words or pecuniary aid.

For the present it is useless to reason with high-caste Hindu gentlemen concerning this matter; they only ridicule the proposal or silently ignore it. There are some among them who would certainly approve and would help to carry the idea into effect, but they must first realize its advantages and see its good results. One must have the power of performing miracles to induce this class of men to receive the gospel of society's well-being through the elevation of woman. Such a miracle I have faith to believe will be performed in India before the end of the next ten years, and if this be true, the enterprise will prove self-supporting after that period with only native aid. There is even now a handful of Hindus entertaining progressive ideas who are doing all they can to reform the religious and social customs of Hindustan, and who will, without doubt, support my work from the beginning; but they have little with which to forward the cause except their personal services.

An institution of the kind indicated, where the pupils must be supported and the foreign teachers liberally paid for their services, cannot be founded and afterwards kept in a flourishing condition without money. Therefore I invite all good women and men of the United States to give me their help liberally in whatever way they may be able for a period of about ten years; it is my solemn belief that it is the most sacred duty of those who dwell in this highly-favored land to bestow freely talents of whatever kind they may possess to help forward this educational movement. I venture to make this appeal because I believe that those who regard the preaching of the gospel of our Lord Jesus Christ to the heathen so important as to spend in its accomplishment millions of money and hundreds of valuable lives will deem it of the first importance to prepare the way for the spread of the gospel by throwing open the locked doors of the Indian zenanas, which cannot be done safely without giving suitable education to the women, whereby they will be able to bear the dazzling light of the outer world and the perilous blasts of social persecution.

Mothers and fathers, compare the condition of your own sweet darlings at your happy firesides with that of millions of little girls of a corresponding age in India, who have already been sacrificed on the unholy altar of an inhuman social custom, and then ask yourselves whether you can stop short of doing something to rescue the little widows from the hands of their tormentors. Millions of heart-rending cries are daily rising from within the stony walls of Indian zenanas; thousands of child-widows are annually dying without a ray of hope to cheer their hearts, and other thousands are daily being crushed under a fearful weight of sin and shame, with no one to prevent their ruin by providing for them a better way.

Will you not, all of you who read this book, think of these, my countrywomen, and rise, moved by a common impulse, to free them from life-long slavery and infernal misery? I beg you, friends and benefactors, educators and philanthropists, all who have any interest in or compassion for your fellow-creatures, let the cry of India's daughters, feeble though it be, reach your ears and stir your hearts. In the name of humanity, in the name of your sacred responsibilities as workers in the cause of humanity, and, above all, in the most holy name of God, I summon you, true women and men of America, to bestow your help quickly, regardless of nation, caste or creed.